A STRANGER TO HELL

by

Stefan Badeni

With an Introduction

by

Jan Badeni

TABB HOUSE

First English edition in book form 1988
with a new Introduction 1988
published by
Tabb House, 7 Church Street, Padstow, Cornwall, PL28 8BG
Previously serialised in English in the *Hibernia* magazine
and in 1963 published in Polish Veritas

Printed and Bound in Great Britain by
Hartnolls Limited, Bodmin, Cornwall.

INTRODUCTION

THE Badeni Family originated in northern Italy and, according to historical and genealogical records, came to Poland in the 16th century with Bona Sforza who married King Sigismundus 'The Old'. Shortly afterwards, in 1563, they received the Polish patent of nobility.

The Badenis seem to have made no particular contribution to Polish history until the latter part of the eighteenth century when two brothers, Martin and Stanislas, gained prominence at the court of the last king of independent Poland. Martin achieved the position of Minister of Justice and was later the author of the constitution of the Polish state known as the Congress Kingdom because it was created by the Congress of Vienna in 1815. Stanislas acted as private secretary to the last king and was known to be particularly trusted by him. His charm and manners were proverbial and gave birth to the Polish saying 'polite as a Badeni'.

The family was not at all numerous but throughout the nineteenth century almost every member of it was notable, earning ten entries in the Polish Biographical Dictionary. They reached the height of their influence at the end of the last century when Poland was partitioned between unneighbourly neighbours, Russia, Germany, and Austria. The only part of Poland with some semblance of freedom at that time was the autonomous state of Galicia (part of the Austro-Hungarian Empire). Stanislas Badeni (father of the author of these memoirs) was the all-powerful head of that state, while his brother, Casimir, was Prime Minister in Vienna.

This combination gave for a time an extraordinary power to the family, with one brother at the helm in the province while the other could influence directly the course of decisions taken in the Empire's capital. The position was noted not only locally but throughout Europe where a number of jokes and poems referred to it in France and Germany. One of these referred to Galicia as 'the great principality of Badeni-Badeni' as a paraphrase of the well-known principality of Baden-Baden.

In the relatively short period between the first and second World Wars the world and the attitude of people to each other changed considerably. The not too taxing adventures to which Stefan Badeni, as a young man, was subjected in the first war contrasted strangely with the inhuman treatment he received in the second. Of course a man's social position was then still of importance as the following short resumé illustrates.

At the start of the 1914 war Poland was still partitioned, which meant that Poles were drafted into opposing armies and often members of the same family were required to fight against each other. It was not then entirely clear what would be the most patriotic course to follow as all sides made promises of freedom for the Polish nation.

The early stages of the war between Russia and Austria were fought in the traditional and panoramic pattern of Napoleonic battles. The trench warfare of the western front was still far away. At the early battle of Krasnik, in which Badeni took part, huge cavalry forces in colourful uniforms faced each other, charged and counter-charged, the sword of the Hungarian hussars against the Cossack lances, while the Austrian generals gathered on a dominating hill to survey the scene, discovering only too late that their purple-lined capes presented an excellent target to modern weapons.

The Russians advanced deep into Galicia in the early months of the war, and Badeni's main estate, Koropiec, was soon behind their lines. It was then that a rather extraordinary thing happened. Stefan Badeni obtained leave from the Austrian Government to visit his estate in enemy territory. He first went into Roumania (then neutral) and from there to Russian-occupied Galicia. His carriage and horses met him at the station and the Russian HQ staff, who were living in the castle, immediately vacated two or three rooms that he usually occupied. He then proceeded to administer Koropiec, unhindered until the Austrian counter-offensive made significant progress. The Russian sector commander now became worried that with the proximity of the front line Badeni would be an embarrassment, and with many apologies he told him that he would have to be deported. If he wished, he could go to the Ukraine, where most big estates were owned by the Polish aristocracy, provided that he gave his word of honour not to leave without permission. A Cossack was assigned to him as both guard and servant; he took his duties seriously, but the latter more than the former.

"While I slept," Badeni recounted afterwards, "he invariably stretched himself on the bedside rug and never failed to address me as 'your brightness', which was the correct Russian style in speaking to a count."

Badeni remembered the months spent as a 'prisoner' in the Ukraine as one of the happiest and most care-free periods of his life. The great hospitality of the Polish land-owners, some of them relatives and all of them friends, and the enforced lack of all responsibilities created a happy background as long as his funds lasted, but some time in 1916 these ran out.

Badeni considered what to do. The Commander-in-Chief of the Russian southern army was then the famous General Brussilow, and Badeni decided to request an interview with him. He travelled to the General's Headquarters, rather uncertain whether the extremely busy commander would even be willing to see him. This apprehension, however, was soon dispelled. An ADC politely explained that the C-in-C was at a conference that morning in the map room but that if Badeni cared to return in the afternoon he was sure the General would make time available.

When the interview took place the Russian Commander was friendly and courteous to the Austrian subject. "As far as I can see," he said, "the front line runs right through your estate at the moment and it is rather doubtful if your land is providing any income at all, but if you come tomorrow to see my Army Paymaster I am sure something can be arranged."

The Paymaster, a jovial, bald-headed colonel, had some prepared documents on his desk the next day. "The only thing I can do for you, Count," he greeted his visitor, "is some compensation for the cattle we had to slaughter at Koropiec. I have here a list of the beasts and their dead weight. This was, of course, a pedigree herd, but I am not allowed to take that into consideration. You can, however, claim in due course from the Ministry of Defence. I have here 30,000 roubles which is the equivalent of the carcase value of your herd. If you care to sign this receipt, the money is yours."

Badeni's sabbatical could thus continue until the advent of Kerenski.

It would be necessary to have lived through the early days of the Kerenski Government to understand fully the extraordinary feeling of exhilaration and rejoicing which gripped all classes and nationalities composing Russia. "For my freedom and yours," was everybody's cry. Spring was everywhere. The long Russian winter was at an end and the ice on the rivers was cracking at last. No one, apparently, could forsee the flood of desolation and misery that would ensue.

Rules, laws, and regulations were swept aside, and Badeni returned to Koropiec. The castle, incredibly, was still standing, but all the furniture had gone, chopped up for firewood during the previous winter. The front was again approaching, this time with the Russians in full and final retreat. Badeni lodged with the parish priest (always inseparable from his parish) in the spacious and well-appointed presbytery. They could hear the guns rumbling in the distance and, on a fine and cloudless afternoon, Badeni used to recall "I went for a walk with my host in the fields beyond the church. We could see for a great distance from there and, after a time we noticed an extraordinary scene. A line of men, walking abreast and spaced every ten or twenty yards, as at a great shooting party, appeared on the horizon. As they came closer, we distinguished Russian uniforms. It was not a battle, however; no shots were fired. Fascinated, we watched as they closed in. An officer and some soldiers approached, guns at the ready. "We are looking for deserters from our army. Who are you? Deserters or spies?"

Badeni explained who they were.

"Anyone can put on a priest's habit," was the answer, "and if you were really the landowner you would have been deported."

A lengthy argument developed. At this stage of the Russian Revolution, officers were no longer in full command; justice or injustice tended to be dispensed summarily by a unit committee.

"We shall have to consult and decide how to deal with you," the officer explained. They were left under armed guard while a group deliberated for some time within earshot. They were lucky! The committee commissar explained in a typically Russian fashion: "The incident is liquidated". They were free to go home.

That night and the following day, Russian troops rumbled through the village. Messages which filled them with ever greater apprehension were brought to the presbytery. They were transmitted somehow by word of mouth from village to village, as happens in time of war, with a speed at least comparable to the telegraphic system

5

of the day. The Russian rearguard, they were told, was composed of totally undisciplined units. Rape, murder, and looting were commonplace. Officers had fled in fear of their lives and had been replaced by ever-changing revolutionary characters. The two men waited anxiously through the night.

The Austrian gunfire was getting closer as dawn broke. Occasional rifle shots came from the village. It was 6 o'clock in the morning as Badeni lay in bed in the presbytery and heard an ever-increasing thunder of running boots.

"They were now in the garden, in the house, on the stairs; then my door was flung open. The first soldiers paid no attention to me but only quickly scoured the room for money and valuables and rushed out. The late-comers were more thorough in their search. After a few minutes everything had been taken that could be of any use. Occasionally, an insult or a threat of execution was thrown at me. I was not particularly frightened; the fugitives seemed in too much of a hurry to bother. They disappeared, as they had come, with a thunder of running boots, and it seemed as though a whole regiment must have passed through my room in that hour of dawn. Then silence fell. We were in no-man's-land, without possessions but safe."

The Austrians seemed in no hurry to advance. They subjected the village to a lengthy though rather inaccurate bombardment, hoping, no doubt, that when they eventually arrived their adversaries would be completely gone.

The Austrian general, when he arrived, exclaimed, with some dissatisfaction "How is it that your house is standing? We had reliable information that the Russian HQ was based there and it was subjected to a thorough forty-eight hours' bombardment."

"I said that I was sorry," Badeni related, "but that really I was pleased; a point of view that he eventually

6

understood."

Peace came, but not at once, to a Poland that was again independent. Badeni married, but then came the siege of the town of Lwow during the Polish-Ukrainian War at the time when his wife's first child was being born there; and then the Bolshevik invasion – miraculously repulsed by the Poles – which just preceded the birth of their second child. Then real peace at last; all eighteen years of it in which to rebuild and heal.

The task was immense. Estates had been ravaged and capital totally devalued by the galloping inflation that came after the war ended. The main resources available were faith and will power, and Badeni applied himself whole-heartedly to the work. Within years, results could be seen, and by 1939 Koropiec was not only an example of a prosperous agricultural and forestry estate but also widely diversified. Badeni produced there 2% of the Polish hop crop, ran a spirits refinery, a fish farm, a 300-acre fruit farm and vast nursery gardens. Also high-quality grass seeds were produced and two herds of pedigree cattle and a remount stud maintained.

To manage such a huge administration a large labour force was necessary and this, in turn, imposed responsibilities, ties and burdens from which Badeni never shrank. A great part of his income went voluntarily to charitable and welfare institutions for which he felt as responsible as for his own family.

One other important part of the author's character should be mentioned and this was his great love of, and interest in, nature. Travelling through the woods and fields at Koropiec, he had constant opportunities to observe and admire. He enjoyed shooting, but, although he was a renowned shot, it was not his skill as such for which he loved those days of recreation. He published a book on the subject between the wars in which it can be seen that he wrote much more as a naturalist than as a sportsman.

After his years at Mauthausen he never killed. "I saw too much of it then," he used to say. "The flame of life is precious to all who possess it. If I am bothered by an insect, I never kill it; I just encourage it to go away."

Thus passed eighteen years of hard work against a background of a deeply happy home life with his wife and children. Then, on 1st September, 1939, came the German invasion of Poland and on the 17th the Russian invasion from the east which had been secretly agreed with Hitler. On that warm, sunlit September morning, we heard that the Russian army was advancing into Poland and would reach Koropiec within hours. We hurriedly packed a few things and left. All that Stefan Badeni had built up with so much care was lost that day.

Our crossing of the border into Hungary is the opening point of the book. It may be of interest to relate briefly here some details that the book does not tell. From Budapest, my sister and I left to join the Polish fighting units in the West, and, a little more than a year later, my mother died in Budapest. My father was in constant touch with the underground resistance in Poland. He knew Admiral Horthy, the Regent of Hungary, and had considerable influence with him from the days of the Austro-Hungarian Empire. He was thus able to give valuable help to agents coming out of Poland to Hungary (then neutral) or going from there into German or Russian occupied Poland. Hence the Gestapo interest in him, his arrest and imprisonment.

Stefan Badeni's faith and principles were so strong that nothing that happened to him could overwhelm him. Misfortunes seemed somehow small, and the spirit with which he resisted his persecutors is recorded among the notes concerning him in the infamous tale of Hitler's rule at Mauthausen. 'Under interrogation he gives insolent answers.'

When, at last, he was freed by the advance of the Allied Armies in the spring of 1945, he at once wrote to me

8

through a Polish liaison officer in Austria who apparently knew me. The letter travelled for some weeks. It was written in the faint and uncertain hand of a man whose physical strength had been all but extinguished. It ended 'I am happy that in the autumn of my life I was allowed to experience such an adventure'.

In fact, the doctors did not expect him to survive, but his remarkably strong physique triumphed and he slowly recovered. When he was well enough, Badeni settled in Dublin and there he devoted himself to his old love – the reading and writing of history. His articles were published regularly in *Wiadomosci*, the Polish literary weekly that circulated among exiles all over the world, and soon he came to be recognised as one of the leading Polish writers.

When this volume was published in Polish, it was reviewed in the *Polish Daily* by the well-known author Maria Czapska. 'I have never met,' she wrote, 'with a description of an internment camp such as that written by Badeni, and yet I have read many and reviewed many – Polish, French, German. His is that of a man who believes in God, who is prepared for death, a Pole wanting to give proof of it and not shrinking from the tragic fate reserved for Poles. The shouting of the guards, their crazed looks, their dirty language, the roll-calls, beatings, death sentences – he saw it all, coming within a hair's breadth of death in the gas chamber. But this was not what held his attention. He looked upon the problem of crime and outrage as an evil unavoidable in a concentration camp. He saw his oppressors as a fierce pack of wolves, tearing their victims to pieces, or as beings ruled by laws and impulses quite unknown to him. What he sought, and what he managed to find in the camp, were traces of kindness, mercy, courage, sacrifice; the pastoral work of the camp chaplains, the dignified attitude of those sentenced to death, the flashes of humanity sometimes seen, even in the eyes of the "wolves".'

Upon those who knew Stefan Badeni in those last years,

his absolute serenity made a deep impression. This aging man to whom Fate had dealt such terrible blows, this exile in a foreign land, had a contentment rarely found in more fortunate men. "You cannot imagine," he said, on one occasion, "how happy I am to have no possessions."

He died on 16th August, 1961.

I

PRELUDE

"IN a few days," the officer said to me, "the Russians will get to this frontier and then the band will start to play." He quoted this German saying in the original tongue, pronouncing it with a strong Hungarian accent. He was the commander of the border guard at Koromezo; the date was the 18th September, 1939, and I was crossing the frontier into Hungary as a refugee from eastern Poland into which the Russian armies were now advancing.

Obviously the officer had no political sense if he thought that Stalin would invade a country which basked in the protection of Hitler, and the average Hungarian had, indeed, no fear of this happening. They were, however, worried from the first days of the war that the protector himself might take over their country in order to harness it to his total war effort. This fear was certainly intensified when the roads from Poland streamed with refugees and fragments of military units after the September disaster and when, by every forest track and mountain pass, young men were slipping over the frontier bound for the Polish Army in the West.

This migratory movement was to last throughout the war, but it was at its peak in the first two years. It was not difficult to recognise these new arrivals in the streets of Budapest, to some of which they gave a different character. Some of these escaping Poles, instead of travelling further, settled in Hungary to ensure lines of communication between their country and the Western Allies and to promote other anti-German activities. This was no secret to the German minister. He raised his voice,

11

he complained, he threatened. Then the authorities would close, for a while, all routes leading to the West and those who did not want to wait for their reopening had to use their own resourcefulness to continue their journey. Not a few examples of stubborn persistence shone in those days. I remember two young men, for instance – Jack Debicki and Stanislas Gut – who travelled to Istanbul, a journey of fifty hours, by clinging to the underside of a railway carriage.

The Hungarians did not stint in giving all kinds of help to the Poles, but there were also sometimes incidents of a different nature when the Hungarian public helped the Gestapo to hunt down the fugitives in the streets. This, however, was not frequent. The Poles were a dissonant element and the Hungarians often recognised their superiority over themselves in matters of ingenuity and enterprise; they told the story of how an arrested Pole was bound and, for security, put into a sack by two policemen. Next morning found the two policemen in the sack and the Pole gone.

Those of our hosts who were on the side of the Germans knew how to combine their beliefs with a certain sentiment for us. They regretted that we did not know how to agree with the Germans and concentrate our antagonism against the one great enemy of us all – the Russians. They had never forgotten the words of the Russian General Paskiewicz to his Czar in 1849: 'Hungary lies at the feet of your Imperial Majesty'. Seventy years later, the regime of Bela Kun acquainted them with the methods of Communism.

The political friendship of Hungary with Germany was a tradition. In 1897, Kaiser Wilhelm II visited Hungary and, with the great spontaneity and actor's intuition which were part of his character, made himself immensely popular, answering the drab and colourless toast of Franz Joseph with a speech worthy of a Hungarian patriot. The enthusiasm of the Hungarians, which was beyond

12

description, led them to call one of the main boulevards in their city after him, and so it remained, despite the course of history. Hitler was a less comfortable friend than the Hohenzollerns, but the growth of his importance in Europe meant for many Hungarians the growth of their hope of regaining the territories lost through the Treaty of Trianon in 1919. "If we follow Hitler we could gain a lot," some of them said. "Yes," replied others, "but we would lose all. We would be ruled by the German Ambassador."

The official policy in the early part of the war followed a line of careful friendship. The views of the Hungarian people were divided. Among the aristocracy, which still preserved its ancient influence, there were some (those supporting the return of the Habsburgs) who were outspoken opponents of Germany, while the others continued to regard the Germans as policemen of Europe, watchdogs of the established social system. The middle classes were quite friendly to the Nazi ideology as they frankly disliked the Jews and hoped to inherit their position in commerce and wealth. Hitler had also a number of friends among the military, for the German laurels attracted the generals.

Among the intelligentsia – the professors, scientists, writers, many of the rich business people, all those to whom freedom of thought was the greatest treasure – the arrest by the Nazis of university professors in Krakow made a deep impression. The position of the Socialists who ruled an adroit press was as clear as that of the Jews. They felt themselves to be Hungarian patriots. The richest among the Jews, Chorin and Weiss, carried great authority with the community socially and politically and they were acknowledged even by their enemies to be enlightened and extremely beneficent men.

The Poles arriving in Hungary were united by one all-pervading feeling – an overpowering bitterness that the struggle of the army had lasted so short a time. Our hosts noticed with astonishment that the refugees mentioned

13

any personal loss only casually and as an inevitable consequence of the tragedy of their Fatherland.

Shortly after his victory over Poland, Hitler spoke to the German people. For the vanquished he had only mockery and contempt and he repeated an old and fine poem, shouting over and over:

Mit Mann und Ross und Wagen
*So hat sie Gott geschlagen.**

The blasphemous reference to the will of the Almighty, those *'gesta Dei per Germanos'*, we were to hear later in all his speeches in the years of his triumph.

During those early days there was inactivity on all fronts. A Hungarian diplomat returning from London told me of a conversation he had had with Churchill, then First Lord of the Admiralty. "You Hungarians," Churchill had said to him, "I am told you are friends of Hitler. Pray do me a favour. Tell him to bomb London and then some of these fools here may understand that there is a war on."

After the fall of France and the resulting enthusiasm in Germany, when all the films and photographs of these events were widely circulated in Hungary, many a moderate Hungarian reflected that a cause carried on with such vigour and ability might perhaps be a just cause, and there were few people in the country who did not believe that England would be brought to her knees wihin a couple of weeks. "How much of a chance do you give England now?" I was asked ironically. "Only 50%," I used to say, "because 15% must be allowed for the possibility that Hitler is an incarnation of the Devil and has supernatural powers."

The days of the greatest anxiety came when the British airmen, together with many of our own, snatched from the German air force the victory which they had almost had within their grasp. At the same time the Hungarians were

*With man and horse and waggon
God has struck them down.

14

passing through a period of great elation. Their friendship with the Germans brought them a magnificent gift; the lands of Transylvania which they had lost in the Treaty of Trianon were now, under German pressure, returned to them – 44,000 square miles.

Soon, however, Ribbentrop was to present his bill; the 600,000 Germans in Hungary were to be allowed to form an autonomous unit and Hungary had to join the German-Italo-Japanese Tripartite alliance.

Count Teleki was at the helm of the Hungarian Government to which he had been called by the Regent at the beginning of 1939. He had replaced ministers who were prepared to co-operate more closely with the Germans. He had been brought up in the ideas of the nineteenth century and had had a partly English education; he was a highly esteemed university professor of geography, a sincere Catholic and a man of good heart. Towards us Poles he was very friendly and it is worth noting that he refused the German request to use parts of Hungarian territory during their invasion of Poland. Now, with a heavy heart, he had to agree to German pressure. As a counter-measure he instigated the last independent Hungarian political act; this was a pact of friendship with neighbouring Yugoslavia. Soon, however, in the early spring of 1941, this matter took an unexpectedly dangerous turn. Hitler sent a letter to the Regent of Hungary informing him of his decision to over-run Yugoslavia and demanding co-operation and free passage for his troops. The Hungarian Government felt bound by the recently concluded pact, and Teleki expressed himself against the German request; then news came to him that General Werth, a Hungarian of German origin, had already agreed to all the details and the time-table without reference to the Government. In the face of this treacherous act, and under pressure from all sides, Teleki said to his ministers "I have done all I can. I don't know what else I can do."

15

During the night, he wrote a letter to the Regent and, as I heard afterwards from his friends, also one to the Pope. Next morning the Hungarian radio announced that the Prime Minister had died tragically. That day the ministries and Government offices of Buda were covered with black flags, but none of them could match the darkness that filled the hearts of the Hungarian people. No other suicide could have made such an impression as the departure of this quiet, unassuming, honest Prime Minister.

Within hours, the awakening town heard the rumble of German columns racing along the Danube. German planes dived low over the roofs in a manœuvre now familiar all over Europe.

The Regent sent to Hitler's High Command his Minister of Defence, Bartha, with a declaration that across the still-open grave of his Prime Minister he could not agree to the German invitation to join them in an assault on Yugoslavia. Hitler accepted his message, but, turning to one of his assistants, he expressed himself unable to understand these Hungarian scruples.

The suicide of the Hungarian premier was looked upon as an atonement to Yugoslavia and the world for the breaking of a promise. I believe that this is not a full and adequate explanation. The idea of suicide is alien to a Catholic because it is the negation of faith, but within the framework of faith there are examples of sacrifice and immolation. I felt then that Teleki gave his life for the future good of his country and, at peace with his conscience, he went to the Supreme Judge. This act, however, was neither remembered nor even mentioned at any conference table and the Hungarians were abandoned to the one enemy they had feared most throughout the last hundred years of their history.

The year 1943 started for Hungary with a military catastrophe. On the distant snows of Woronez they lost half of their divisions and nearly all the heavier military equipment. Shortly after this, I got an unexpected invitation from the Chief of Staff, General Szombathelyi, to go and talk to him. He seemed changed since I had last seen him, and the events of the last weeks were marked on his features. He started by pointing out that all the Poles accused of spying had recently been released. Later, he spoke of the traditional friendship between our two nations and he assured me that I could always turn to him with confidence. In return he asked me if I could try to influence my countrymen in Hungary against taking any unwise actions.

From the very start of my exile in Hungary, I used to see a great number of people from various social strata. Everywhere I talked about German atrocities and our stand against them. As I spoke aloud and with emphasis I felt that I was not contravening the law which forbade whispered propaganda. A year or two later I was to be told in the central office of the Gestapo in Melinda Street "Yes, we know about you. You have spoken widely against us."

A frequent subject of discussion at this time was the attitude taken during the war by the Holy Father, Pope Pius XII. My Hungarian friends who knew my great attachment to the Church knew, also, that I had to a certain extent my own views on the subject. I used to say that they did not need to convince me. I knew that the Pope not only had a lot of warm words for us in his encyclical 'Summi Pontificatus', that he not only administered a very severe reproof to Ribbentrop when he received him in audience, but also that in every material sense he was helping us where and how he could. I go even further in my homage to him because I believe that he would gladly have given his life for suffering Poland. But I did believe, in spite of all this, that a painful discord in feeling had arisen between Pius XII and my country. We had expected that the Holy Father would, at least momentarily, descend from the heights of his throne and

17

his world-wide diplomatic responsibilities and would speak words that would identify him with us, pointing out to the world quite clearly what atrocities were being perpetrated and by whom.

Two great shocks awaited us in the summer of 1943. First Katyn. Does the faded, powerless word 'crime' belittle what took place near Smolensk? Some Hungarians thought that the Germans could have done these deeds but *we* knew whom to accuse. The blackest deeds have their different faces, their different character. Over the pits of Katyn hung the spirit of Asia, the bloody cruelty of the Mongol, so horrible that it was difficult to believe.*

The second event, the death of General Sikorski, made upon us in Hungary a strong impression. The General was such a warm patriot and he was so Polish both in his qualities and his defects that for that alone he was dear to us. It was sad, we thought, that he would not see the day of victory.†

Then better news reached us – the Italian debacle. But the fate of Italy seemed to strengthen the argument of those Hungarians who believed that they should persevere on the side of Germany. "Look what happens! The ancient king bravely and adroitly dismisses Mussolini. The Italians surrender and wish to throw themselves into the Anglo-Saxon arms but they get no help from them. Their proffered hand is rejected and nothing is done to aid them against the fury of Hitler.

---

* In the spring of 1943, the Germans, advancing eastwards, discovered in the woods of Katyn, on Russian territory, mass graves of 4,800 bodies of Polish officers. The Russians claimed that the massacre must have been done by the Germans. However, an international commission of neutral countries established beyond doubt that the Poles had been murdered three years earlier, in the spring of 1940, when the russians had disposed of the Polish prisoners whom they held in camps in that area.

† After the discovery of the Katyn mass graves, the Polish Government in Exile, headed by General Sikorski, asked the Russians for an explanation. This was refused, and diplomatic relations between the two countries were severed. General Sikorski was a particularly awkward person for the Russians to deal with as he had an established rapport with both Roosevelt and Churchill. A place carrying him on the return journey from the Middle East to England crashed on take-off from Gibraltar, and it was alleged that sabotage had been engineered to eliminate him.

They are only mocked."

The Hungarian Prime Minister, Kallay, an honest and decent countryman, had based his policy on the now very probable victory of the Allies and on the promises of the Atlantic Charter. Now, with deep anxiety, he noted the declining influence in Europe of the Anglo-Saxons and the daily increasing influence of Russia. When he turned to the West, looking for understanding, he only met, every time, with the request for unconditional surrender and this, for the Hungarians, did not mean a surrender to the armies of the West which were hoped and longed for, but a wide open door to Russia and Communism. The BBC programmes directed to Hungary were so clumsy and offensive that not even the most ardent Anglophiles could bear to listen to them.

While the brows of Hungarian politicians darkened, life in the country still flowed with ease. The economy, helped by the richness of their agriculture, was still sound, and the restaurants of Budapest were always filled, not so much by the hungry as the greedy. The tempo of social life had not slackened; at receptions the latest jokes about Hitler were passed round. Many were amusing, but the partisans of the Germans listened with studied solemnity and only observed that these must have been invented by the Jews.

One evening in September I was reading quietly at home when I was told that "a very suspicious-looking Pole", wanted to see me. A moment later, I looked at the tall figure entering my sitting-room. Could it be from Poland? Could it be Prince Andrew Sapieha? I could not make up my mind. If it were he, then he had grown older and greyer. The stranger stood in front of me, looking uncertain, asking if I recognised him. I looked at his shoes which, although much used, were obviously made by a first-class shoemaker. I greeted Sapieha and we sat down. He had been sent by the Polish underground headquarters and he wished to contact the Hungarian

Chief-of-Staff. He had been told by his superiors "Go straight to Badeni. We are sure he will help you with everything."

Two days later, I saw General Szombathelyi. He noted for his staff the assumed name that Sapieha was using and told me "Yes, of course I know the Sapiehas. They are like the Esterhazys are to us," mentioning one of the great Hungarian names.

A few days later, Sapieha and I were waiting in the ante-room outside the office of the Chief-of-Staff. He had been receiving several German generals and, as the door opened for their departure, we watched with amusement their noisy and boisterous farewells. We were the next in. I introduced Sapieha and left, reflecting, on my way home, what a variety of visitors the Hungarian Chief-of-Staff received.

I also introduced Andrew Sapieha to Count Bethlenem, the influential elder statesman, and Sapieha reported with pleasure to his headquarters in Warsaw the speedy establishment of his contacts.

It was soon after this that I was invited to join a commission of three people whose task it was to countersign the accounts of the Polish underground army in this sphere of their operations. As I worked through the mountain of often trifling bills, I smiled at the thought of how gladly our brave secret couriers quenched their thirst in the strong drink of their enemies. We were told that the certification of these accounts would be photographed and reduced to a microscopic film so that it could be hidden for safety and one day placed in the museum of the underground army. For our own safety, we were advised, we could use assumed names for our signatures but, spurred by the prospect of fame in the museum, I signed very clearly my own name.

Winter was already ending and the days of ease in Hungary sped by. Their futility seemed to weigh upon me and I felt the burden of my stories about my country, my boasting in the drawing-rooms of Budapest always of someone else's distant heroism.

I knew, somehow, that the end would be dramatic, for the Hungarians as well as for the Poles in Hungary. I felt, as never before, the advent of an adventure. And it was logical, it was just, that I should have to give some better proof of my beliefs than mere words. Would I – badly prepared by an easy life which I had always been able to order to my own will – would I manage as well as those in Poland? What was going to happen to me would be a due paid late to my name and position. I hoped that I should be able to remember this in the hours of reckoning.

II

THE FIRST ENCOUNTER

IN the early morning of 29th March, 1944, I had a telephone call from my friend Gratz, a politician and parliamentarian, who asked me to come and see him immediately. We sat down in his drawing-room and he announced to me that at this moment the German mechanised columns were approaching Budapest. "This time," he said, "it is not a rumour. Hitler is the master of Hungary and we are in the power of the Gestapo."

I thanked him for thinking of me at this moment and told him that I should not bother to hide. I returned home and started the dreary and unpleasant task of burning any papers that could be considered compromising.

From how many chimneys in Budapest that Sunday did similar smoke rise into the sky? On the ground, signs of trouble were plainly visible. The traffic, normally light on Sunday, was very busy, many a sleek limousine travelling at a speed far beyond the prescribed limit. The head of the Government, Kallay, number one enemy of the Germans, fled to the Turkish Legation. Many Hungarians made for the country. The members of the secret organisations had, many of them, hiding places prepared for such an eventuality, but some less prudent found themselves in a quandary. They tried to efface their tracks by changing apartments or hotels or arriving with a suitcase at the house of a friend where they were not always greeted with enthusiasm. The Germans were to seek them out, one by one, all through the spring, and then often the host as well, although impeccable in his attitude towards Hitler, would be imprisoned for good measure.

The first to be arrested were the important Hungarians, according to the list long ago prepared by the German Embassy; democratic politicians, monarchists, the Jewish élite, several generals, and scientists. The Gestapo acted according to the rules of their art, rushing into apartments, shouting, threatening, brandishing pistols, sometimes shooting. There was not, in all this, the slightest element of real anger. They played at terror, for this good acting insured them against military service at the front. Not a few who were arrested, seeing by their side a German fuming, raving, and gnashing his teeth, imagined the cause of his excitement to be their own importance as an enemy of Hitler, but the German was usually thinking at that moment of what he was going to eat for supper and how he could amuse himself that night.

I lunched in the Gellerta Hotel that Sunday with three other Poles. Next to us there was a table of Gestapo men. This was the first time in my life that I had seen them. They behaved exactly as if they were at home. Perhaps among them were our future persecutors, for two of us who sat at that lunch were soon to be shot by the Gestapo.

I had tea with Hungarian friends, as was my custom on Sunday. Already the first stories about arrests were being passed round. The member of Parliament Zsilinszky (Smallholders' Party) had defended himself and was grievously wounded. Chorin had managed to reach an airfield and had escaped to Switzerland. (I recalled a similar story about the Viennese Rothschild during the Anschluss.) In one house, two spaniels, excited by the turmoil started barking and were also, apparently, shot by the Gestapo. Two elderly ladies, who for years had heard my stories from Poland of German persecution and oppression, eyed me fearfully. "How can it be that you have not yet gone into hiding?" they exclaimed. "The best place is a convent. Go to a convent." It did not occur to me at the moment to reply that I was not Ophelia.

Next morning I went straight to the office of the Polish

23

emigrés in Budapest. I felt in an excellent mood. Perhaps it was the carefree mood of the condemned man which, like sleep, is a gift of God. On the first floor I touched the bell. The door opened instantaneously and the hands of several Gestapo officers reached out for me. "Please do come in. We should like to have a little chat with you." One of them put his hands lightly on my shoulders and deftly moved them down each side of my body to see if I was armed.

I was taken to the Astoria Hotel, which was the headquarters of the Gestapo during the first few days of the occupation. Walking in a leisurely manner between two Germans and exchanging a few words with them from time to time, I must have looked more like an informer than a prisoner. The day was wet and I had my umbrella with me. Later, the Governor of the prison was to tell me in a moment of graciousness "You with the umbrella, you look just like that Chamberlain."

My arrest took place, if one could say such a thing, in pleasant circumstances, but my arrival at the hotel was like a jump into cold water. The hall and the restaurant were teeming with Germans. The hard Prussian accent echoed everywhere. Bursts of laughter erupted frequently. The Germans were in a mood of elation in this newly occupied capital, rich in food and full of nightclubs and wealthy Jews. Hands shot up in the air constantly and on all sides. "Heil Hitler, Kamerad!"

I was taken upstairs, floor after floor. Accustomed to lifts, I found it a difficult journey. My fur coat, too, seemed inordinately heavy. My escort, however, was not sadistic. "The heart is not doing well?" he asked me. "Then let's stop and have a breather."

On the top floor we entered a room. A few young men sat behind a table, writing. "Hey, you! Shut the door there!" The tone of voice, even more than the words, brought me face to face with the reality which had now started for me. In my whole life no one had ever spoken to me like that before. I had a childish impulse of revolt. Closing the door slowly, I said, ironically, "But of course. With pleasure." The Gestapo man looked at me. Then he smiled, came towards me and said in a very low voice, "But what's the matter? Why are you so easily offended? Don't we two want to keep on good terms? Don't you agree?"

After he had taken my particulars and asked a few questions, we went down again but instead of stopping on the ground floor we went on towards the cellars. "What is this?" I thought. "Will it be the torture chamber already, so quickly?" It was not as bad as that, but the sight which I saw I shall never forget. In the big underground ballroom there were about three hundred people. They sat or stood, but all were silent and motionless. The gravelike stillness in the dim hall packed with people made a great impression on me. All the faces were turned towards me.

A chair was found for me. Near me I saw a Polish priest; Count Apponyi, a monarchist; General Keresztes-Fischer, the military adviser to the Regent; Chorin, who I had earlier been told had escaped; Laky, the Minister of Food; and a well-known Socialist, Buchinger, with whom I had dined only a few days before.

We remained there throughout the night. Next morning, an officer of the Gestapo came in with a piece of paper in his hand and read out twenty names – nineteen Hungarian and my own. The Hungarians were the most important of the people assembled there and I therefore duly appreciated my inclusion with them. We were to be taken as hostages who would be shot in case of any sabotage. As we left the ballroom, all eyes followed us with expressions of emotion, and later on I was told by a companion in a prison cell who had been present that day, "When they were taking you away we whispered to each other that you were going to your execution."

In the street a prison waggon with no roof awaited us.

To enter it was a feat of gymnastics and, once there, we had to climb over various chains. The waggon was subdivided into tiny metal compartments and each person had to force himself into the one allocated to him. We waited for some time. Count Apponyi, son of one of the greatest Hungarians, took off his hat so that he would be recognised by the passers-by, but most of them rushed past trying not to look. Only one elderly lady stopped and looked in bewilderment, then raised her hands to her face and walked away weeping.

Atlast the waggon moved, and we travelled to the Fö Street prison. The lower floors were occupied by common criminals. They took us to an upper floor that was silent and deserted. Each one received a separate cell, and soon I was fast asleep.

Surprisingly, there was no sabotage and none of us was shot. We were not, however, released, and three days later we became again ordinary prisoners of the Gestapo.

III

THE CHIVALROUS SS MAN

AFTER that Fateful Sunday in March, 1944, when the German troops occupied Budapest, the spacious prisons of the capital of Hungary became filled to overflowing with people of various nationalities and of every social class.

In a smallish cell of the huge building in Fö Street, twenty-six of us were immured. The first weeks were the hardest to bear, for the Gestapo had placed us under the direct control of Hungarians of German nationality, adolescent recruits in SS uniforms, whose foul words were spoken in voices still childish, and who tried to express their zeal and to prove their maturity by tormenting us. They would visit us constantly. Having entered the cell, one such soldier would triumphantly feast his eyes on us, the enemies of the 'Führer', rendered harmless at last. Then, invariably, he would utter the command, "*Hinlegen! – Auf!*" over and over again. And in the dead of night this "Down! – Up!" would disturb our sleep.

Prisoners of Jewish nationality had an even worse time. We were treated with brutality, but they – who deserved nothing but compassion – with a more intense cruelty. Frequently, in helpless distress, we would listen to sounds of torturing in the neighbouring cells.

After one particularly sinister night, it seemed to us that the very day was dawning disheartened and tired. Early, even before the carraway seed soup and the bread were distributed, the horn of a lorry that used daily to take a few score of prisoners for investigation sounded shrilly in the courtyard. The long corridors of the building sprang into

27

life at once, keys rattled in locks, heavy doors were opened and banged. Our cell, too, was visited by the Governor of the prison, a stocky, strong man, originating from East Prussia, whose tiny eyes glared with the fury prescribed by regulations. One of us remembered having seen him play, one of a visiting team, in a football match in Poznan, and we had all admired his agility and his kicking power. He was fond of beating women. As the head prisoner of the cell, I had much to do with him. Unable to remember my surname, he used to address me by my Christian name. He would show me certain consideration. Once when he thought that some answer of mine deserved reproof he aimed a powerful kick at my shin with his heavy boot, but checked himself so efficiently that he hardly touched my clothes, and I had to look down hurriedly in order to conceal from him an unwilling glance of approval. Now, standing in front of us and mispronouncing our names, he was reading them out from a list, and, shouting fiercely, he was urging those whom he had called out to hurry as fast as they could; to a priest he dealt out a blow. Those who were called out must stand with faces to the wall, lined up in the corridors. Today, I was one of them. When the Governor saw me beside several Jews, his racial heart was moved to compassion.

"But Stephen, don't stand like that amongst these Jews. Move on – there – a little further!"

At last we started, to the rhythm of the heavy footfalls of the guards, the rattling of rifles and the words of command. It took a long time to descend the stairs, hung with prints of pious pictures by means of which the Hungarian authorities had endeavoured to move the obdurate hearts of Hungarian thieves. Our Saviour was opening His arms to a repentant sinner, the Queen of Heaven was treading down the head of the serpent, and St Peter was drowning. These splashes of colour were pleasant to the eye, by now grown accustomed to the

28

drabness of walls variegated only by tiny dots – squashed bed-bugs. I used to look forward to seeing St Peter on the waves of the Lake of Genesareth; this picture was my only contact with nature at this time. I would stare in delight at the dark green depths, foaming prettily, in which the first Apostle was plunged up to his pepper-and-salt beard.

We came out into a small side-street. From a safe distance a group of passers-by watched us with timid curiosity while we were being loaded into a car – not an easy achievement for the car was very high. Inside, on the other hand, it was so low that one had to stand almost bent double in a darkness tempered only by a few rays of light stealing through chinks in the wooden walls. When we picked up more prisoners from the Zrinyi Street prison close by, the car was over-crowded.

Suddenly I heard someone whisper in French: "Badeni, is it you? I am Madame de Dampierre."

"Oh, dear Madame, what a coincidence!" I whispered back, startled at meeting in that miserable vehicle a countess to whose childhood the cedars of Lebanon had sung, and who in recent years had been moving with dignity in the drawing-rooms of Budapest as the wife of the French Minister.

Madame de Dampierre went on whispering in low and wistful tones, which might have been taken for a lament coming from a soul in Purgatory who, in the darkness of the night, was begging for prayers. I learned that never since the beginning of the world had the wife of a diplomat been treated so disgracefully, for she had been thrown on to bare prison boards. Here I put in that we had been given ten – by mistake I said mattresses instead of palliasses.

"Mattresses? Is it possible? Oh dear, oh dear," she moaned, and went on to tell me that these wretched boards made her head, her neck, her back ache . . . in one word she was sore all over.

Meanwhile our car laboured uphill, precariously

29

swaying sideways and giving violent jerks; but those on their way to Gestapo interrogations were indifferent to such things, being about to receive treatment which might vary between the offer of a cigarette and the adoption of violence to enforce speech.

The car stopped, and we were herded out. We were now high above the city in Melinda Street. This name, so pleasant and sweet, is reminiscent of honey, and yet what a bitter meaning it acquired during the year 1944! How many people will shudder even now on hearing it mentioned! We entered the comfortably-furnished hall of a large building which, until now, had been a hotel. The regulations provided that here, too, we should be lined up along the walls at a distance from each other, like naughty children. But we happened to have exceptionally kind-hearted guards; nobody shouted at us when, rapidly, my lady companion and I made for a large sofa. Madame de Dampierre fell on it and sank into its soft cushions with a moan, I never knew whether of pain or delight. She said she wanted to sleep, get lost in oblivion, quit – if only for a moment – this world and all its horrors. But though she prepared to sleep, careful nevertheless that I, too, should sit in comfort, we continued to talk. She gave me her handkerchief to be dipped in cold water so as to assuage the pain in her throbbing temples. She then took a rusk out of her bag and gave it to me; it was the only food I had had for thirty-six hours. In return, I came to her rescue with my comb.

Our conversation in French attracted the attention of the head warder, a simple soldier, very young, almost a boy, who observed us with curiosity. He had a pleasant, dare-devil expression, and on hearing his accent I knew that he was an Austrian from Styria. With intelligent and inquisitive eyes, he watched my companion whose sharp rather Rameses-like profile was now ennobled by suf-fering. He looked at her smart brown suit, at the turban lightly swathed round her ebony hair, which showed threads of silver here and there. When she left the room for a moment, he snatched his opportunity and asked me: "Who is that lady?"

Hardly had I begun to speak when he exclaimed "I see! They could not find the husband, so the poor woman has to suffer!" And, giving vent to his indignation, he bemoaned her fate aloud. I tried to explain to the tempestuous defender of women that the Count de Dampierre came from a country in which the wife, the child, the cook, and the lapdog were not all arrested because of some transgression of the master of the house and that the Count was sure to move heaven and earth to rescue his wife when he heard of her arrest.

The Countess looked much better after her return. Her hair was beautifully tidy, and she was so fresh and neat that she made me think of those aristocrats of the French Revolution who, in their ghastly cellars, remained as distinguished, refined, and meticulous in every detail as if they were about to step on to the parquet floors of Versailles instead of the boards of the guillotine.

I was called up for interrogation. It was my first one here and it proved to be in keeping with the mood of that pleasant day. My questioner, a police officer, politely offered me a chair; there was no rubber stick lying on his desk, nothing to be pushed under my nose as was frequently done before an investigation, much in the manner of a sportsman before a shoot in order to restrain the keenness of an over-eager pointer. For four hours I was made to lecture on the history of my family under the Austrian occupation of Poland, and on my childhood – an angelic pastoral, as even Hitler might admit.

The lights were turned on in the hall by the time I came back and the guards had changed during my absence. Madame de Dampierre met me with a gentle word of reproach for having taken so long. However, she had not been left alone. Count Louis Salm sat on the sofa beside her, an obese, elderly man, a tennis ex-champion, only

31

recently arrested and consequently brimming over with news from the world. He offered me charming blue and gold cigarettes in a most elaborate case, probably a trophy of some successful tennis tournament. As I do not smoke, I declined with thanks. Afterwards, in my cell, I had to listen to bitter words of reproach on this score. "*You'll* never make a prisoner," said a young man from Lwow, who was thoroughly acquainted with prison life. "How could you! You should have grabbed the lot and brought them to us!"

A moment after the discovery of this careless refusal, however, I redeemed my character by fulfilling other duties to my fellow prisoners. A Pole came back from investigation. A few days before, he had been taken from our cell in order to separate him from his friend. The lives of both might perhaps be saved if the other knew what this one had said. Notwithstanding the shouts of the guards, I made my way towards him and learned by heart a mass of unfamiliar names and involved particulars. One special detail stuck in my memory because of its flavour: "I met X at Y's at an Epiphany doughnut party..." I sighed, thinking of the pleasant days in Hungary when people conspired among doughnuts while searching for the bean which would make them 'King of the Feast'. At night, on our way back in the overcrowded van, I was still learning my lesson from my teacher and was therefore unable to keep Madame de Dampierre company. But we left the van with a warm handshake and wished each other "*Bonne chance*". My 'good luck' to her proved the more effective. Soon she was set free. Her 'Hungarian Rhapsody' was published immediately after the war, with an account of our meeting in the prison's box-like van.

I seemed to have lost sight of the chivalrous Styrian. He was not present during my next investigation – a terrible one this time. A few weeks later I was taken to another cell in which, for the second time, I was elected head prisoner. My imprisonment continued, but it would be untrue to say that I suffered in the Budapest prisons. There I learned by experience how little physical discomforts really matter if the morale is good. I felt at home in the company of young people, mostly gay and inclined to joking. We had good relations with some of our gaolers, but derived more enjoyment from our squabbles with the SS men. Our sense of discipline slackened, and we gained the reputation of being the most cheeky cell in the prison. Less and less frequently would I call out "Attention" on the entry of a soldier, and my companions would line up implying by their every movement that they did this as a special favour. At the time, we still nursed the hope of the war soon coming to an end and of our returning to our own country, free at last.

I well remember Wednesday, June 7th. The deep blue radiance of the sky lit up even our cell, shut in by walls. On Wednesdays we received our food parcels. On that particular day, the first recipient shook the sausages and the strawberries out of the latest newspapers in which they were packed, and read out to us that Rome had fallen and the invasion to which we had looked forward so much had begun.

Soon afterwards, I had a pleasant surprise. I met in the corridor my friend from Melinda Street, the Styrian. He at once exclaimed that he had met me in the company of the "French countess". He was now head warder in our prison. He began to visit us, invariably friendly and polite. He would smile kindly as we passed down the corridor on our way to walk in the tiny courtyard, walled in and smelling of the laundry fumes on one side and of kitchen odours on the other. On Sundays and feast days, when the Governor would leave the prison early in the morning to go to a party, the Styrian would open the door wide so as to make it possible for us to listen to the Mass which was said on one of the upper floors for Hungarian prisoners. He would then slip up and down the corridor as quietly as possible, cap in hand, and we would kneel at the sound of the Sanctus bell and listen to hymns beautifully sung by criminals and to the sermon of a courageous Hungarian chaplain who, instead of preaching on the seventh Commandment, thundered away against those who trampled down the dignity of man.

But day after day went by and the invasion made no progress. Also unwelcome changes occurred in our prison life. Our food parcels were cut down. Our favourite game of 'words' began to lose its attraction; I began to feel the dearth of topics for my lectures which had been a great success with every prisoner, without exception, for while some had been interested the others had gone pleasantly to sleep. The shortage of cigarettes was a real tragedy. A pinch of shag rolled in a piece of paper became a treasure, and I watched in amazement the same tiny stump pass from mouth to mouth for an equal share of whiffs, passionately inhaled.

At last, on a certain Sunday afternoon, when even the patch of sky visible from our cell loomed leaden, we admitted to each other that prison life was becoming increasingly boring. Someone added that Sundays in prison were more boring than any other day. I remarked that a new, tough SS man would wake us up. I must have said it in a good moment, for immediately after this the key rattled in the lock at an unusual hour and a strange soldier with an evil expression appeared in the doorway. He at once shouted "What does this mean? Have you given up calling out 'Attention' in this cell?"

"Yes," I admitted, good-naturedly, "we have given up calling out 'Attention' in this cell."

"Bloody Hell!" he shouted, as he went out. "I'll see you later."

At once, I said to my companions "If he comes back I will call out 'Attention' and, gentlemen, you will be kind enough to line up according to regulations, but if, in spite of this, he is out to torment us and orders 'lie down', I won't do it whatever happens."

My plan was accepted, and we waited impatiently for the friction likely to take place. An hour later, the soldier found us in perfect order. He looked round for a long time; at last he yelled "Lie down". I remained motionless at the head of the row, and the dead silence behind me proved that we were unanimous. I have never in my life seen such stupefaction as that exhibited on the face of the SS man. He would sooner have expected the building to crumble than not to see us face downwards on the floor. At last he spluttered out "What does this mean? Don't you understand German? Down!" But a row of statues faced him. "Who can speak German here?"

I volunteered.

"Well then?"

I said that I had called 'Attention' and my colleagues had lined up according to regulations. There was no reason for ordering 'down' and we would not carry out the 'down'.

Excitedly, he went out into the corridor and, violently gesticulating, called for someone to come.

The Styrian, whom we had not seen for some time, appeared. "What is happening here?" he asked, greatly surprised. I told him and once more repeated that we would not lie down.

"Well then, I'll have to report this to the Governor." But his voice sounded kind. He did not report us and he ordered the other enraged soldier to keep quiet. And so it came about – a most infrequent, perhaps even a unique occurrence during Hitler's twelve-year-long omnipotent rule, that a group of Gestapo prisoners who blatantly refused to obey orders met with no reprisals. When, soon afterwards, the days of our Hungarian Aranjuez came to an end and we became acquainted, in Upper Austria, with the terrible reality of the Danube quarries (where the slightest sign of disobedience meant death in torture) we would frequently express to each other our surprise that our flagrant resistance in Budapest could have been left

35

unpunished. Only here did we appreciate in full the noble deeds of the Styrian soldier. And later on, when prison and camp had withdrawn into the past and I was regaining health and strength in beautiful and peaceful Carinthia, I would carefully scan the newspapers to see whether I could not come across the name of our defender amongst the SS men now imprisoned and awaiting trial. I would fain have become his defender then. But it was not given to me to repay that debt of gratitude.

Perhaps that chivalry of his which had made him sympathise aloud with the tormented woman, brighten our days and conceal our revolt, had also kept the young Styrian faithful until the very last to the crumbling standards. Perhaps he was one of that handful of Germans who fell fighting to the end amid the ruins of the Royal Castle in Buda.

IV

DURING THE AUGUST HEAT

THE advance of the seasons of the year was pleasantly marked in Budapest prisons, where one day differed little from another, by the varying kinds of food parcels sent to us by our friends. To begin with, these were delivered four times a month, afterwards only twice. Spring radishes somehow failed to give us pleasure; the June strawberries, on the other hand, were more than welcome. The beginning of July was marked by cherries, round and firm; and after the apricots came the first apples. This meant August.

For a long time, our group had been left alone in the cell, but it had begun to dwindle rapidly during the last few weeks. A soldier, card in hand, would enter, shout the names, and add "Take your *klamotten*, look sharp!" Those called would hastily tie their bundles and boxes while we surrounded them, trying to instil into them some hope that they were going to be 'set free'. Then the door would bang after them. For an hour or two, they would be kept standing in the corridor, their faces to the wall, silent and lonely, as if recollecting their transgressions. Later on, all traces of them would be lost and they were heard of no more.

It was with strange feelings that I used to look at the empty places left by those with whom we had lived so closely for many months. They had added their voices to ours in conversations serious or gay, in jokes, perhaps even in quarrels, transient as a storm in June; and, all of a sudden, as if surprised by an unfriendly gust of wind, they were swept away from among us by the single word of a

37

soldier. Where to? Not to freedom. Perhaps to 'free labour'? Or, in all probability to their death because of some sentence passed somewhere upon them. And if to a camp? Would they still be able to fight for their existence in tolerable circumstances, or would they suffer cruelly under inhuman conditions? Should I see them again? Here, between these narrow walls, they had been thinking their thoughts, their feelings intensified by the long period of tension; part of their souls must have remained amongst us – and yet how silent, how mysteriously silent they kept!

In August, the rumour spread through the prison that no more deportations would follow. Those who had not left by this time would remain the prey of the Budapest bed-bugs till the end of hostilities. We turned a willing ear to this news, for it would be pleasant to be set free here where we all had friends, relations, and possessions. It was true that, at the last moment, before this would come to pass, the SS men might shoot us, or set fire to the building, or blow us all up, but this we simply had to counter with the words "it will work out somehow . . ." The only thing to say in a situation like ours.

During the night of 16th-17th August, some three hours after midnight, the key turned in the lock. As I was lying nearest to the door and was a light sleeper, I awoke at once. This was the hour of departures and I felt that my fate had been decided. The NCO turned on the light and read out first the name of the priest, mispronouncing it. The priest had taken a sleeping draught an hour before and now Morpheus did not release him; he was reacting in an unorthodox manner, for which he was rebuked. When the NCO began to mispronounce the second name, I interrupted him with the word "*Hier*".

Much pleased, he commended me and quoted me as an example. Never had praise given me less pleasure. While I was saying goodbye, two of my now former companions were beside me, ready, in this hour of need to help and give advice – a colonel and a nineteen-year-old boy from Cracow; they obligingly packed my numerous odds and ends.

As I was passing the office, following the soldier, I made an interrogatory gesture towards a Jewish prisoner who was working there. He did not utter a sound but moved his lips so expressively that even a loudspeaker would not have given me better information: Mauthausen. I knew about the camp only from what a judge had told one of our prisoners during an enquiry: "You will probably go to Mauthausen. It is a beautifully situated place. The air is very good there."

After standing for a long time in the dim corridors, we were driven, squeezed tightly together in cars, to the Keleti station. It was neglected and sordid and by now rather damaged by bombing. Tired people watched us with boredom. In the cattle truck, into which enough light penetrated through chinks and holes, we numbered – besides the soldiers guarding us – over twenty Poles, Hungarians, and Jews. We sat down on the floor; the officer who accompanied us made himself comfortable on a small bench and spread out a newspaper with headlines which were as triumphant as if the year 1944 was a year of German victories. The officer was not a bad man and shared his joy with us. "Seven hundred V-1s a day fall on London," and after a moment he exclaimed once more "And soon we shall have V-2 as well, to which the other is child's play!"

Beside me sat a young Pole of perhaps eighteen. He found himself in prison for having served as courier between Poland and Hungary. I was delighted to hear that he, like myself, came from the southern provinces of Poland. I asked about possible common acquaintances, but he knew nothing. We became friends, however, and I gave him a piece of bacon which a generous Hungarian had lavishly bestowed on me, and he, in return, offered to help me carry my things. The hours in the stuffy truck

39

dragged on as slowly as did the train itself.

Amongst us was one prisoner who was the governor of a bank and who had lived in opulence for seventy years. Now ill, almost unable to move, he suffered a hard deal at the hands of fate. At some station he peered out through a hole and, raising his arms, drew back with a cry. The ghost he had seen was the inscription 'Totis', the name of a village where stood a castle of the Princes Esterhazy in which he had often stayed in happier days. The rest of the company tried to shorten the time as well as they could. The Polish temperament did not give in. Several young men beat time on some chance instruments and hummed gaily as if they were recruits going to join the army, or even students on holiday, but certainly not Gestapo prisoners on their way to a place of annihilation.

At dusk, we reached Vienna. Memories revived in me. Vienna was at her most charming in the last century, when she had a certain rhythm of her own, a special tone not to be heard in any other capital. That tone was given by the incomparably swift tapping of the horses' hooves on the asphalt as they drew the graceful Viennese carriages. I did not expect that this ancient Vienna would greet me here with any echo of the past, but an officer of the Gestapo came to our truck in order to check us – an old, good-natured Viennese. On hearing my name, he was visibly moved and repeated it several times, looking at me in a friendly fashion.

The train did not leave the precincts of Vienna but it was on the move the whole night, either advancing or retreating, shunting with jerks of the trucks and squeaking of wheels. Attempts at sleep made us more tired than keeping awake. At dawn we were taken to another train and to a third-class carriage. How pleasant it was to have a seat and what joy to look out of the open window! For five months I had not seen space or inhaled fresh air. We were passing through a forest. I have always been in love with the charm of forests and there is not a single hour of the twenty-four that I have not, at some time or other, spent in their midst, gun in hand. I cannot measure the time passed in thickets or the distances trodden under vaulting of the trees. All that happened in the far-off forests of my own country. But now this foreign forest enveloped me with its friendly, sylvan breath, spoke to me with the cool fragrance left by the night's imprint on the soil, the damp hazel twigs, the pine needles. And it was not only a glimpse of the beauty of God's nature that I perceived as I sped swiftly past on my way between the two prisons. I also caught sight of man-made beauty. I saw the splendid baroque Melk Abbey on its high granite rock, standing guard over the Danube. This sight was familiar to me, as was also the neighbouring district of the great Austrian lakes, gleaming with the bluest of smiles between their high mountains.

We changed trains at Amstetten. My young friend, who was walking beside me, kept on muttering in tones of reproach that he would have escaped this morning "if it had not been for these things of yours!" However, he would flee at the next station. I answered that this morning, too, I would have carried my things willingly had I known. I was interested. Would he succeed? When a prisoner escapes, the SS men, instead of commending the other prisoners, usually take revenge on them for their own lack of supervision. Prison ethics, however, perfectly fair, permit everyone to have an equal chance of saving himself. When we got out at St Valentin I lagged behind a little, my companion following, empty-handed this time, the guards walking carelessly on either side of the road. Luckily, there was much movement in the fairly large station; trains were drawn in, empty coaches stood about. I listened in great tension. Everything was quiet behind me, so either he had given up his idea and had not attempted to escape, or else the beginnings had been successful. When we stopped, I realised with satisfaction that he was not there. The soldiers checked us once, twice,

41

three times. At last, one of them hurried to the commandant and another began to swear at us. "Now, if you arrive there without him, you wretched lot, you'll get a good hot supper! They'll break every bone in your bodies!"

The commandant, not so very angry, asked me how the escaped man was dressed and what were his particular distinguishing signs. He had, in fact, been wearing a blue suit and a brightly coloured pullover. Pretending that I was trying to remember, very slowly – for every second was valuable – I told them that he had worn something greyish and that there was nothing to distinguish him from anyone else.

The local police started in pursuit, and we entered another train. I was very tired. Although before my arrest my weight had been normal in proportion to my height, I had lost thirty kilograms in the cells, for I had been eating only the things I liked. While I had been in prison I had felt very well with this loss of weight, had enjoyed my sudden lightness and listened with pleasure to the governor of that prison when, looking at me with angry eyes, he said "You grow younger every day!" Now, all of a sudden, we were made to undergo a great physical strain and effort, and I saw the other side of the picture. The swellings caused by hunger from which I had suffered in prison now increased greatly. We had to endure extreme thirst, and the heat was intense. The heat wave this year justified its reputation.

The train stopped. The painter who, years ago, had painted Mauthausen on the station building, did not know what he was writing. At that time, this name, pleasant in itself, suggested only customs duties collected here in former days, probably some farthings and coppers. In the middle of the twentieth century, another kind of customs duty was exacted here and from all over Europe.

Having got out, we were kept standing in the sun for a

42

very long time. At last the commandant got into his car; the bank governor, by now only half alive, was pushed into another car amongst some cans, while we were formed into rows of five deep, that notorious formation in which, in camp, even dying men were forced to drag themselves into gas ovens. The hour was early afternoon and cinders seemed to be falling from the skies. We were told the distance was only five kilometres, but it was increased by the heat, by our fatigue, and by the bundles which we carried. Arrested in March, I was wearing a heavy fur coat and carried two bundles. My neighbour in the row was helping not only myself but also the priest on my other side, and his strength soon failed. By a lucky coincidence, a convoy of Russian prisoners-of-war overtook us. These unfortunate men had nothing except a few rags on their backs and their stomachs were empty so they were only too eager to take our suitcases.

The road led slightly uphill; from under the numerous feet clouds of dust arose. The little Austrian towns had not changed since the time of Franz Joseph – the same, invariably yellow, low cottages, with a great many shop signboards and here and there a balcony. The streets were empty; the heat had driven the inhabitants indoors, or were they avoiding the sight of us? I tripped over a stone and fell down. The young soldier close to me perhaps felt some pity. "This one cannot go any further," he said hesitantly. But the older one laughed carelessly. "If he can't walk then he must be threatened."

We were allowed to rest in a wood, and we sat down in the shade as if on a picnic. I think that there was even a stream murmuring close by. After a few moments we arose once more.

By the simple means of such marching, an uncanny result was achieved. It was with joy that we greeted the sight of the camp when it appeared in the distance. I, at least, looked with sincere pleasure and with curiosity. What did a concentration camp look like? Perceiving

43

wide, sunny spaces, and groups of low wooden buildings surrounded closely by fencing with timber turrets at intervals on which sentries probably watched day and night, I told myself it was a border outpost, a *fortalice*, as it was called in ancient Polish, and this beautiful word out of past centuries and historical novels imprinted for ever in my mind the first vision of my Upper Austrian destiny.

V

THE BEAUTY OF MAUTHAUSEN

THE prison and concentration camp adventure through which I lived in the autumn of my life seems to me today as a sort of cinema film – improbable, strange, and undoubtedly shattering, but interesting, too, full of colour and meaning. It seemed improbable, for I had grown up amongst ideas infinitely remote from everything it represented. I had read about gory persecutions endured for patriotism's sake in former days, inhuman prisons, inquisitions and tortures, and was filled with due respect and admiration for heroism, but I had considered that, on its present high level of civilisation, mankind had left these things behind for ever. When human frenzy let loose in the middle of Europe brought back that world of cruelty, it engulfed me and a host of others. My thoughts then turned back to those impressions I had derived from reading, and I lived through those experiences, so novel to me from the very first, in a literary manner as well. I looked from that angle at our persecutors during the dramatic moments of questionings and investigations, in everyday prison life which – with its customs, slang and, frequently, even gaiety – reminded me of my school-days,and also during the long, hard months of the concentration camps. My imagination comparing, shaping and beautifying, created for me a special romanticism of captivity, and this, added to the consolations of Faith, greatly helped me to live not without serenity through that episode of my life.

It is not the place here, in a brief chapter, to ponder the meaning of suffering in the life of an individual. For many reasons, I do not look back on my experiences as on a nightmare to be shaken off. In fact they were less terrible than the fate of many other Poles. I remember with gratitude the many human kindnesses I received in the camp. I could never forget, even if I wished, that prisoner from Lodz – under twenty – who saved bits of bread from his scanty ration to buy me shoes. Or that old man from Konin who, likewise, provided for me at the time of my greatest poverty. Or his companion from Gostynin who, trying to conceal what it was all about, would battle with the stern Spaniard dealing out the soup in order to get a little extra for me. I can see clearly, even now, the silhouette of the Wilno undergraduate who, having made my acquaintance, kept on visiting me in hospital as if it were his duty, boring though it probably was for him. He was the more welcome in that he arrived in the forbidden morning hours. Though many must go unmentioned, I cannot leave out that priest from Czestochowa diocese who was a stranger to me and who, from his distant barracks, found me on Christmas Day "so that I might hear the Word of God from somebody's lips". Several times, my partner in political conversations, Joseph Putek, gave me friendly help. But my chief benefactor was a man from Lwow, one Witold Nowosad. We came from the same city and we were both interested in history. Witold it was who, on a Saturday preceding the entry of the American armies, saved me from the gas chambers by sheer intuition and the promptitude of his action.

Now and then, under the impact of strong impressions, the beauty of soul in one prisoner or another would reveal itself to me. Frequently one would chance to enter into conversation when passing with some unknown prisoner, one of the many thousands, and at once his very first words would reveal an unusual mind, understanding, ideas in common; and one would have liked to prolong, to renew, the conversation which was usually forbidden, stolen at some risk, but this one could never do. Today,

46

the name has long ago faded from memory, the features have been blotted out; he had not survived, perhaps... and nothing has remained but the memory of one such single precious moment, shining like a jewel in the setting of gloomy days in the camp.

WHEN after a laborious march under the hot August skies, my companions and myself were approaching the camp and saw its gate, Dante's by now rather trite description never occurred to me. My impressions were mainly coloured by the afternoon hour, the not yet finished harvest, the landscape breathing contentment, and most of all the deserted-looking gate thrown wide open as if in hospitality. But hardly had we passed through that gate, than we found ourselves in the very midst of camp impressions. The *capos** surrounded us in a noisy crowd. What would a Hitlerite camp be without the *capos*! How difficult to imagine! They gave the camp its atmosphere, its special character. They did us no harm at the time, though the history of the camps teaches that the *capos* and the SS men would have liked to join forces to let newcomers have a foretaste of what was awaiting them. However, we were not to be received into the daily life of the camp by such an initiation; only by yells and lusty though innocuous swearing did they instruct us in our duties of the moment.

Covered with dust from head to foot, but so far clad in an opulent manner, luggage in hand, we presented the picture of a caravan of travellers attacked by a gang of robbers. We were lined up under the notorious wall, while even more important *capos* faced us, seated officiously at their little tables. We were to hand over to them everything we possessed with us and also upon us. It could all have been done quickly, but in the camp all things proceeded in a complicated manner based on a

* The *capos* were prisoners who by collaborating with their captors by informing on their fellow prisoners and in other ways, earned special privileges for themselves.

47

number of illusions. Huge sacks made of excellent paper were brought and each of us had to throw his things into a separate sack. Then they were tied and labelled while we had to sign repeatedly for small trinkets put into envelopes. Sometimes one of the *capos*, a man with a particularly degenerate face, would provoke us menacingly: "You think, of course, that we are going to steal all these things?"

After this not exactly cheerful joke, which was the final farewell to our possessions, we were like new-born babies, entering on a very new life on some other planet, and as such we began our existence with a bath. The pipes in the bathroom did not whistle and let out gas, but showers of pleasantly warm water. Having then passed through the hands of barbers whose agile and well-practised hands shaved us and attended to us with meticulous care, we received our clothes - not, alas, tidy canvas suits with beautiful blue stripes, but a variegated heap of rags which had been torn off corpses innumerable times. A pair of clogs, badly in need of repair, was thrown over to me. On my way to the distant barracks, I was recalling the pictures of paupers I had seen before. Now, in these rags, weak, emaciated, swollen with hunger, carrying my clogs in my hand and trying to avoid the sharpest pebbles on the road, I could have won in any competition as to who looked the most destitute, as was the habit of beggars when they gathered round churches for some great festival.

Near the barracks I met an acquaintance, a Hungarian aristocrat. At my request, he brought me some drinking water in a bowl, the first I had drunk in fifty hours. With a feeling of indescribable delight I took that cool treasure into my hands. It was evening and the roll-call was over, and it felt like recreation time after school hours. We entered the barracks. As my Hungarian mentor was explaining to me in beautiful French the topography of the barracks and the time-table of the day, I could well

48

imagine that I had arrived into the castle of his ancestors, and when, with normal good manners, he introduced me to the more 'outstanding' prisoners, I almost felt like a guest of some distinguished club.

We were to sleep on the floor in one of the two halls. This would not have been so bad, but how many square metres were we allowed and how many hundreds were we? How many of us were to share one mattress? Has any painter dared to throw such an orgy of bodies on to his canvas? I was ordered to lie down next to a wall in a corner; this was an evident smile of fate. For though timber pressed against me mercilessly, at least while pressing it did not maintain that I disturbed it and prevented it from sleeping. My hardships in this respect were only physical, and that was a great happiness in camp. My sleep was a kind of contest of an overtired organism against everything else. But after midnight I lay wide awake.

Guns were heard and after a moment I also heard the purring of approaching aeroplanes. Both sounds were rapidly increasing. The firing grew intense and the purr of planes became a roar. Suddenly lights shone all over the camp and, slowly descending, they surrounded it with a flamboyant wreath. Now, all at once, we became untouchable, although our lives a moment ago had presented no value whatsoever. The artillery around us went wild. The airmen were now right over us; the attack was powerful, planes came over in unbroken waves and the roar was unceasing. The guns thundered even more loudly, but in an uneven, feverish manner. The firing would cease and then burst out again with redoubled fury. It seemed to me at times that it was a many-headed pack of monstrous hounds guarding our wired-in paddocks, which now tore at their chains and threatened the daredevils who violated the silence of a German night.

The barracks shook and trembled, the wall by which I lay bending now and then, thrusting me aside. But more

49

than the roar of the attack, more than the barking of guns or the fairy-like illumination, I was impressed by the dramatic power of the contrast through which we were living. Here, below, ourselves, the over-crowded, the persecuted slaves, and high above us – distant and yet so incredibly near among the British airmen – other Poles, different from us, free, gay, and victorious. Though our brothers and perhaps our sons are among them, they pass us by, intent only on fulfilling their mission; our longing for them flies upwards together with the German bullets and, together with the bullets, seeks them in space... And we went on listening to the humming of their planes, even, persistent, stubborn, which sounded here in our barracks like the voice of the British Empire itself which, also, could not be forced by anything to deviate from the path once chosen, aiming in the same calm, persistent, stubborn manner towards certain victory. And today, when I think of my impressions at that time, I must admit that that one hour of my first night at Mauthausen was beautiful.

Nights in August are still short, and soon the sharp sound of the morning bell woke some from their sleep. Those whom it took away from their dreams were by far the more numerous. Those who did not sleep were meditating on freedom and its treasures, never before appreciated. After the bell it was impossible to meditate any longer, for all thoughts had to be concentrated on struggling against the many difficulties of the day. The combining of very small activities with very great difficulties was one of the plagues of the camp – one of the milder ones, it is true, but sill an incessant one. Things which would otherwise have no importance here grew into problems.

There were three main reasons for that. The over-crowding and competition, the haste for ever required, though for no obvious reasons, and the presence of the *capos*, always inimical and interfering. To begin with, it was not an easy task in the crowd even to put one's clothes in order, primitive as they were. It was even more difficult to make one's bed and cover it with the blanket, especially as this had to be arranged not only carefully but with great art, under the threat of punishment which could not be taken lightly. It was a feat to push one's way through to the very few wash-basins.

As we were in the quarantine barracks, we did not have to march out into the large square where, twice a day, 15,000 prisoners would line up for the roll-call. We were to line up on the narrow strip of ground between our own and the neighbouring barracks. From there we saw nothing but the barrack walls and the barrack roofs, gates, and barbed wire. The sky overhead was the sole proof of the existence of something else besides the camp. It was a bond between ourselves and the world. Now, high up, small clouds were floating in the azure space – white, sharply outlined. They were tiny signs of lasting fine weather. The day even now promised to be hot but there was a pleasant and refreshing breeze. While we waited we stood and talked in semi-whispers. Although we had only arrived on the previous day, we had already adapted ourselves to the atmosphere around us; we grasped it, we were merged into it, and it was as though we had been here for a long time; nothing surprised us. We understood so well, for instance, that the life of the block-supervisor's she-cat, which now played innocently in front us, was more valuable than that of any of us. We talked quietly and serenely about various things in a leisurely way. Psychologically we had responded to the first impressions of the camp with some sub-conscious patience, indifference, dulled sensibility.

And yet . . .! Under that cover of indifference and dullness, the desire for freedom was smouldering within me, within each one of us – a desire burning white with its intensity. What would have been the outburst of our feelings if news had come suddenly of the collapse of Germany, the end of concentration camps? But nothing,

51

as yet, foretold the imminent approach of such an immense happiness. Our first days were to go by without even any news from the fighting world reaching us. There was a sign, made with the hand and known to all the prisoners, which conveyed from one to another the news of an Allied victory. We did not see that mysterious and enchanting sign, that gesture of strong defiance, symbol of victories, which during this war was perhaps born of the battlefields but more probably in the silent agony of the camps, and which lit so often an ecstatic rapture in yearning eyes.

Our long prisoner files stirred. The moment of the roll-call was drawing near, and we straightened ourselves and lined up beside each other as if with the aid of a yard measure. Soon the figure of an SS man would appear in the barbed wire gateway, a solemn voice would be heard: "*Mutzen ab*" and we should briskly doff our caps – today and many many more times.

How clearly, how tangibly, I can still see our first roll-call, when we stood erect, lined up patiently, and over us stretched the skies, magnificent, infinitely blue, the quiet skies of an August morning, created for joy.

VI

PASTORAL

IF it is permissible to employ commonplace expressions in describing most unusual matters, I would say that the beginning of my stay at Mauthausen was marked by ideal weather. A joyous sky displayed every conceivable shade of blue, adorning itself, now and again, with the white lace of small clouds. The superficial and optimistic impressions of my first few days were that I had found myself in the depths of Africa in a slave labour colony. The heat was tropical; every morning, long rows of miserably-clad figures went out to work guarded by jailers, cat-o'-nine-tails in hand. In the barracks we were crowded together, cramped for space, the *capos* swarming amongst us, well fed, with sinewy arms, in shirts with low cut necks showing a wealth of tattooings. Their lips, fiercely pressed together, opened only to emit swear-words and curses.

Among the Polish convicts I met companions from the Budapest prison cells. They greeted me with joy and deluged me with advice and even more with warnings: "Heaven preserve us! Not a word of politics."

The Hungarians welcomed us with their ceremonious expansiveness. We had frequently ventured to say in Budapest that before victory came we might still meet in a concentration camp. They were receiving great numbers of parcels, so that they at once offered me a pullover, a towel, and a supply of soap. I estimated these objects at their camp value – that is, in the same way that I would have appreciated a gift of farms when in freedom. The chief *capo* of our barracks, a Pole, was very gracious, thanks to my friends' kind mention of me, and bestowed

53

on me a handkerchief and a piece of bread and jam.

All this, however, had no effect on my extreme weakness, nor did it make my swellings go down. I was by then in danger of a phlegmon, an inflammatory tumour. This melodious word, which I had never come across before, did not describe some life-giving mythological deity, but a visitation, dangerous and widespread in the camps. It is true that the general hospital, the so-called *Russenlager*, lay open to me, but there – out of the accumulated thousands of patients – several hundred were killed every week.

There was one harbour of refuge and comfort in the camp, a real oasis of happiness – the so-called Refuge, a small hospital for fortune's favourites. A Polish doctor and the superintendent of my block backed my candidature for admission. A Czech surgeon was at the head of the hospital. The Czechs were always well-disposed towards me because of my name which was popular among them. And so it came to pass that I found myself in that hospital, in the best ward, on the best bed near the window.

Could there be greater bliss after the experiences of the last weeks, than to lie in an excellent bed, breathe in the fragrant air of the neighbouring forest and gaze, even though through bars, into its green depths, awaiting the end of the war expected almost any day, and gradually become less swollen! I felt quite ashamed to be so comfortable. But my colleagues, numbers of whom would visit me after roll-call, would congratulate me without any jealousy at all, explaining that it was my due for I was the oldest and weakest. They would touch the white sheets with respect, looking around them in disbelieving wonder; they would lift the mattress incredulously and press the springs under it.

There were many prisoners in hospital who had been wounded by bombs while working in factories. Irrespective of nationality, they were better looked after,

54

received a larger ration of food and cigarettes. There were six beds in my ward. A German from Hamburg occupied one. He had not been maimed by a bomb; he wore a pink badge, and the camp authorities, either to punish him or for the sake of an experiment, did to him what the unkind uncle of Heloise did to Abelard.

He was of a delicate nature and subtle in his outlook on life. Later on, he rendered me more than one service. The concentration camp, like a Nuremberg shop, dealt in every sort of article, and so we also had a Basque in our room – a fellow countryman of the splendid Borotra. He could have frightened children with his black and withered face, and only when he laughed did one realise that he was good-natured. Beside him was a bandit from the Sudetenland. I would sooner have dealt with any of Schiller's brigands than with him. Once, however, he cooked some kind of cabbage soup and, unasked, offered me some. He and the Basque had everlasting jokes from morning till night about sending each other to the crematorium. There was also a Russian from the Caucasus – of the gentle type of Russian. He asked me to come and stay with him after the war: "You will have everything you like – shooting, bears. One is happy there."

When he had been transferred to another ward he used to come and visit me. "I am sad without you," he would say, "so I came to see you."

My immediate neighbour was a young prisoner with such a Polish face that, without asking, I addressed him in Polish. He gave me a keen glance and bade me relate the story of my imprisonment. Having finished, I remarked that Regent Horthy had obtained from the Germans the assurance of equal and better treatment for Hungarians and for Poles arrested in Hungary. "And so I am a so-called 'prominent'," I said boastfully.

He looked at me in amazement, and having got over his surprise he explained to me under what an illusion I was,

55

how much time, suffering, wits, and luck were needed to become a prominent. And he laughed to himself. "You a prominent! Of all people!"

He was right. I was a pariah. He was a prominent, though he did not say so. I slowly gathered this from his tidy attire and well-groomed appearance, from the many-coloured cushions which were sent to him from the *effektenkammer*, and which he disposed about him in a most fastidious manner. He also had a firm and decided way of addressing us, though he was only twenty-two. I became interested in this compatriot of mine. How had his sensibilities been affected by the terrible five years of concentration camp? I asked him to tell me his story. He came of a family of small tradesmen, satisfied with their modest well-being. During the first weeks of the war, he was beaten and tortured by the Gestapo for having a wireless set, and he was put in prison. Feeling shy and timid, he approached the most conspicuous bandit of the cell and, wishing to introduce himself, he addressed him politely. The hand of the criminal descended heavily on his cheek. "That'll teach you there are no sirs here!"

In camp he went through every form of suffering. He worked in the worst *kommandos*, was punished frequently, the most terribly for an attempt to escape. But the years went by and his fortune improved. Now, as an old convict, he was one of the chosen. While I listened, I could not help admiring his physical powers of resistance, his resourcefulness and cleverness. Not only had he endured but he had grown up and broadened out. Now he faced the further dangers armed with great experience and in excellent physical condition. He told me at length all about the camp, its customs, psychology, its unwritten laws formed by the co-existence of prisoners. I learned that many things habitually condemned in freedom were laudable here, while things respected there were despised here.

The teachings of this young veteran of the camps were

56

invaluable to me, though they were delivered in language thick with those words which, it is said without reason, are unrepeatable. His was more than the usual camp slang and, finding it impossible at times to discover the idea in that jungle of expressions, I would ask him to use fewer vulgarisms for this sole reason. But he would not agree to any concession. He would shrug his shoulders and say "But we are in camp." He was a relentless realist and something of a pessimist. When I made a serene remark and said that death from gas is said not to be terrible, he did not spare his powers of description to deprive me of that illusion. "Besides," he said "there is no need for gas. They'll send you to the *Russenlager*, you'll get an injection of petrol, and that will do the trick."

Once, when somebody described to me the hanging of some of my acquaintances, he listened with disapproval to the conversation which he thought sentimental, and my remark – "Anyhow, they can do no more than kill, and afterwards a better life awaits us" – made him explode.

"What sheer bosh! How do you know that we shall not be even worse off there?"

"But does it not solely depend on ourselves while here?" I said.

He became thoughtful. The camp had shaken the religious feelings instilled into him by his mother. Like many more mature people, he could not reconcile himself to the incongruity of the simultaneous existence of God and concentration camps. He shared the opinion of those who had not given enough thought to it, that the Supreme Being should constitute Himself a guardian of order on earth. I advised him to say a prayer from time to time.

"Oh," he answered bitterly, "when the Gestapo men beat me because of my wireless, I kept on crying out 'Oh, Jesus! Oh, Holy Mother!' and the more I cried the more they beat me."

I was receiving the usual rations, namely, in the morning, unsweetened 'coffee' made from beetroots, at

57

noon a soup of weeds of the season, and in the afternoon a quarter of a loaf of bread, a lump of margarine, and a slice of horse sausage which tasted like damp rubber. This was our twenty-four hours ration. "Not much" the kind reader will perhaps remark, yet in comparison with what we had – or perhaps rather with what we did not have – later on, this was a Gargantuan feast.

Among the weeds of which the soup was composed was orach, or mountain spinach, with which, for thirty-four years, I had been on bad terms as it would rear its head here and there in August from the potato fields which in July had been free from it. Even in the maddest of dreams, it would not have seemed possible then that there would be a time when orach would constitute my only hot dish for several weeks. Luckily, at the time of my stay in hospital, I had no appetite and consumed very little of the weed. Sometimes I was unable even to eat my whole ration of bread. Thus it was no merit that I gave it to my visitors. Some would never accept it, others I had to ask over and over again. On the other hand, they accepted a cigarette willingly for they knew that I did not smoke. They would divide it into tiny bits. My neighbour sharply reprimanded me for such goings-on and bade me force myself to eat everything, so as to build up reserves of strength.

"What an idiotic thing to do to give your bread to those colleagues of yours, or whatever they are! That is the only reason for their intruding upon you like that. Colleagues indeed!" he would mimic me. On one occasion, cigarettes were brought to him. He counted and arranged them. I took my courage in both hands: "I do not smoke but give me one for –". Seeing his threatening look, I quickly changed colleague for acquaintance. But I did not escape a rebuke. I was told that in camp I would be given nothing for anyone else, that I should not make foolish suggestions for I would only harm myself.

"Had you asked for yourself, I would have given you

58

more. As it is . . . well, I'll give you one . . ." (he was not a bad man) "only let this be the last time!"

As a prominent he had the privileges of the 'organization'. He was brought margarine and potatoes, which his partners fried, and after this they would eat from well-filled bowls. He did not offer anything to me. This was unpleasant – first of all morally, but also materially, for my views on potatoes were not the same as on weeds.

It was only in the camp that I learned to distinguish between kindness and delicacy of feeling. A certain Polish magnate of the nineteenth century, philanthropic to the extent of prodigality, described delicacy of feeling as 'the very flower of kindness'. There was no lack of kindness in the camp, but the flower of delicacy blossomed very seldom. In case of real need a helping hand was extended, but the hand was rough. Had I really needed those potatoes, my compatriot would certainly have given me many of them. Had I asked him without really needing them, he would certainly have given me some. To guess other people's thoughts, to forestall their wishes, to flatter somebody's greediness, was not among the customs of the camp. But at the time I was not acquainted with this hard law, and I used to listen wistfully to the praises of the food the smell of which surrounded me. The heat was great outside; when our stove was lit to fry the potatoes on, the temperature in the ward would become unbearable. I used then to think of shareholders who frequently have to pay high prices for the cigars smoked by managers. Here, the prominents were frying and I was only perspiring.

After roll-call, figures would appear round the hospital, terrifying in their misery and emaciation. They were almost 'moslems', the name used in the German camps for those already half dead. They were those who toiled the hardest, perishing daily in masses. Those who were still alive would come here, saying nothing but just staring imploringly. There were quantities of Poles among them. They would devour my cold weeds, and my neighbour, who had been wounded by a bomb and for this reason received larger rations, shared his food with them scrupulously and always remembered them. Once, however, with the gesture of a real *grand seigneur*, he was also lavish towards me. Out of flour, margarine, and beetroot marmalade, which nevertheless was quite sweet, a tall mound of pancakes arose, and my fellow-countryman was the *bon prince* that day. He gave me one after another, and in the evening he indulged in an even more splendid gesture, though with the addition, it is true, of a very camp-like admonition. Somebody brought him an oblong chocolate candy, alleged to have been made in Paris. Against my will, I was to become convinced of its excellence. He bit off half of it, and the other half he pushed towards my mouth with an energetic movement. I drew back abruptly and instinctively but not rapidly enough.

"What?" he exclaimed, indignantly, "you are going to be fastidious in camp?"

He had an authority which was unquestionable. Everybody showed him respect and the man from Hamburg used to say of him in warm tones: "He is such a nice boy!"

I was attracted by his genuine feeling for Poland. I offered to refresh his memory of Poland's history. He accepted this graciously and would remind me of my promise when the lights were put out. And so I would whisper into his ear the stories of our mediæval kings, the surnames of which caused him much surprise. But such a whispered lecture would not last long. Worn out, I would fall asleep before my tutor who, for that short time, had become my pupil.

The nights were very beautiful at that time. Once, I was awakened by a full moon looking across the barbed wire, straight into my face. How many a time in the past we had looked at each other, she because of the perennial order of the universe and I often out of boredom when I had been

60

sitting in the forest, rifle in hand, and the quarry had failed to appear! Now the moon was making a face. Was she shocked or sorry at having discovered me here? For a long time, unable to sleep, I followed her silent course across the sky. Little by little, she freed herself from the barbed wire, caressing everything with soft touches of light, bestowing even on that wire a silvery life of its own. Then, rising higher, she poured her gentle brightness over the roofs of the barracks and seemed to comfort in her arms this sorrowful bit of ground which was soaked, day by day, with the blood of martyrs and scattered, hour by hour, with their ashes.

In that September, 1944, the evacuated population of tragic Warsaw came flowing into our camp. One day long files of women who were passing on the other side of the wire halted near the hospital; the guards were far away. My neighbour, by no means a laggard, was at the window at once; he leaned out, he called to them, he asked for details of the fighting in the capital. To his strategic comments he added flirtatious jokes which awakened gay laughter among the women. The ever-ready replies in feminine voices, so very unusual here, and in the accent of Warsaw, now renewed the pain at the thought of the final tragedy of that splendid city. Warsaw alone, out of all the cities tormented by the Germans, was suffering proudly and with a smile.

I remember that a pair of new pyjamas was brought to my compatriot on that very day, and I can see him now, in memory, as he was trying them on. They fitted perfectly, and there he stood, straightening up his tall figure, his head with the broad shaven stripe of hair stamping him as a convict, bent slightly to one side, examining them with the attention of a real camp dandy – a perfect type of a young prominent of Mauthausen.

I keep him, the stern instructor, the teacher who guided my first steps in the infancy of camp life, in good – even in affectionate memory. It is not only because of his

61

teachings and of the companionship during my good days in hospital. I find it impossible not to be moved at the thought of a Pole who, when hardly more than a child, had been torn from the parental home and plunged for five years into the immense moral quagmire of a German concentration camp and yet had preserved in it his Polish heart.

VII

THE FALLEN

TO this day, when I ponder the death sentences carried out in German concentration camps, I am unable to make out what were the principles which actuated the judges in giving their verdict in Berlin. Probably here, too, as in many another case in Hitlerite Germany, accident was the deciding factor, and each of us convicts had to face the fact that any day he might be summoned to the *schreibstube* and deleted from the books.

Soon after my arrival at Mauthausen, I was enabled, as I have explained, to meditate in comfort in the camp hospital upon my fate.

I had twice undergone investigations in Budapest, in the Gestapo centre in Melinda Street. The first inquiry – mostly about matters relating to the nineteenth century – was a mere trifle. The second concerned my sojourn in the capital of Hungary. This time it was another interrogator and he had an unpleasant face. Like all the Gestapo, he was an actor in dealing with the prisoners. He was even rather a good one, for he realised that trifling methods may bring about good results. During our conversation which lasted for several hours, he shouted only once or twice and otherwise he played with the soft pedal down. He stifled his anger with great effort, he spoke through his teeth, at times he clenched his fist. Neither were his swear-words exaggerated: *"Sie frecher, sie unverschamter Pollack!"* ("You insolent, you shameless Pole!") He regulated the expression of his eyes. From being full of common sense they would become hard and relentless; then they would express hatred, and in the end the interrogator eyed me with disgust.

I felt pretty safe. My partners were not many and from the outset had been very discreet. I trusted that they would not let themselves be caught. The greater part of the conversation was not concerned with any unpleasant subjects; I talked at great length and when, afterwards, the interrogator was dictating my statements to an NCO, I argued about every little misinterpretation. The interrogator began to employ repressive measures, ordering me to take my hands out of the pockets of my fur coat, and then to get up. "As a punishment, you will have to answer standing up." He went on dictating: "Extremely insolent behaviour, gives insolent answers".

If these words were really put down they would constitute a most unpleasant addition to my dossier that would follow me to the camp. Part of the interview passed in profound silence, for the interrogator had, in front of him, incredibly large piles of papers which he perused, and he sometimes spent a long time in looking something up. These pauses were particularly unpleasant. Once I felt cold all over when I heard a pseudonym from his lips which I did not expect him to know. But he mispronounced it markedly and added an invented title of Count, for the Germans like pomposity. So I was able to answer that I knew no such person without running an undue risk of being punished for lying. To other delicate questions, I also gave evasive answers, and he did not insist. I realised with joy that he knew the names but not the facts. He did not formulate any terrible accusations. To the charge of having spread anti-German propaganda, I answered that I had talked of war like any other Pole. To that of having intervened on behalf of my fellow countrymen imprisoned by the Hungarian authorities, I agreed. I satisfied my questioner's curiosity as to what my son was doing abroad by expressing my belief that he had probably joined the Polish Army in England.

The fourth accusation I had to refute, for it would have

brought me too much honour. "You were the Polish leader in Hungary."

I answered that, leaving out of account everything else, it is alien to the Polish nature to have leaders.

The harvest of these several hours must have been negligible, for in the end the judge asked me whether I wished the Germans well. When I answered "No", he exploded with assumed indignation. I asked him whether he wished Poles well; he passed it over in silence. He seemed satisfied and brought the interview to an end. My assertion: "I do not wish the Germans well, I have been their political adversary ever since September 1939," was the last sentence in my statement, which I was then given to sign.

THE first of my companions to be murdered by the Germans was a prisoner who shared my cell at the Fö Street prison. He was the owner of a Cracow bookshop. After I had been sent to Mauthausen he was shot in Budapest. I do not know the reason for this hurry. Others were murdered in fulfilment of sentences passed in the camp. This was the fate of the five Poles who had been working on a Budapest Committee. Hardly had these luckless men arrived in Mauthausen when the sentence of death by hanging was read out to them.

No small sensation was created by the appearance in the camp of five of our officers sent here from a prisoner-of-war camp. Amongst them was Colonel Witold Morawski, whom I had known for a number of years.

Poles in Mauthausen who had access to the stores did not like our officers to undergo the humiliation of rags and clogs, and they endeavoured to get them better clothing. A convict tailor quickly made a navy blue cap in German style, and Witold came to see me in hospital. He told me at once that he considered his own cause lost. "I know the Germans," he said. "I do not expect a lenient verdict." He was forty-nine and longed to go back to life which, until now, had been so generous to him.

He promised to pay me a call every other day, but soon took to coming daily and bringing many others with him. He would take the place of honour on the only stool. The others sat close together on the edge of my bed and on those of my neighbours without ever asking permission, in the manner of the camp. Others stood wherever they could. There would be a babble of voices and we would even be gay at times. There were crowds, for everyone eschewed the atmosphere of the barracks and, besides, the hospital was considered to be an excellent source of news from the fronts – good news, of course, for no one would come to listen to it if it were bad.

The crowd around me attracted attention, and once, before nightfall, the hospital *capo* reprimanded me; of course, not in a discreet manner but after the habit of all *capos*, especially the German ones, in shouts: "An SS man tells me that every evening the whole of Poland gathers around you and that you all talk politics nineteen to the dozen!"

The reprimand was not severe, but the idea of the SS in connection with the word politics was simply equivalent to being murdered in camp. This was very menacing. In consequence I had to ask my friends to limit their visits to me. Thus I could now talk to Witold with greater freedom. We did not talk about the camp; we preferred topics which took us far away, and especially into the past. We would talk of shooting, the charm of which sport appealed to us both alike, of farming in the south east of Poland, frequently of mutual friends already departed and about whom no one in the camp knew except the two of us.

But now and again he would become silent and cast down. "Yes, my case is an ugly one," he would say. "Nothing but a speedy victory could save me."

Then I would recite to him all those cheering items of news which, acting as an injection of hope, simply maintained life in many of the prisoners. I told him about a descent from the air near Hamburg, of unheard-of numbers, about the Rhine having been crossed in seven places at once, about the fall of Karlsrühe, the threat to Frankfurt-on-Main. But he was not one of the credulous. He was always serious, he would never laugh gaily, but notwithstanding this he would invariably sit and talk to the very last minute that he was permitted to stay.

We had two sad evenings after the days in which our friends had been executed. The first victim was a young Pole who had been imprisoned in Budapest. I made his acquaintance only during the hard days of our common journey to Mauthausen. He used to come to see me quite often, and sometimes would drop in just for a moment, even before roll-call. During one particular nocturnal investigation, it was he who was torn at and dragged about by a wolf-hound at the notorious wall. The wolf-hound belonged to the Deputy Commander, Bachmeir, who personified the entire horror of the camp. The boy would not cry out because he knew that only when he had done so would the torturer call the dog back and set him on the next victim.

My companion was even more shaken by the sentence passed on a young priest who had offered all the burning enthusiasm of his soul to Christ and his country. Witold had made friends with him and would stay with him whenever he could. The young priest blanched a little when he was summoned, but with firm steps he walked towards the other Polish priest in the barracks and knelt in front of him, asking for his absolution and his blessing. No one approached death in a more beautiful manner. To him, it was drawing nearer to God. He was murdered by a shot in the skull. Both these sentences, as well as subsequent ones passed only on Russians from our barracks, were carried out on Wednesdays. This established the conviction that there was no danger of being called to the *schreibstube* on other days. When, after

67

the afternoon roll-call, the critical day was as good as over, Witold would say, with a sigh of relief, "I have another week to live. Meanwhile perhaps something will happen on the front."

But, alas, nothing ever seemed to happen. It was Aachen and Düren, and Düren and Aachen, over and over again.

November began. All Hallows Day was warm, bathed in sunshine. On All Souls Day, autumn began its cold, sleety reign. An icy wind chilled us to the marrow of our bones, entering through broken window panes, and the leaden days dragged on. Witold came to see me daily. In November, a certain friend of Witold's was admitted to the hospital. On November 8th, a Thursday, early in the afternoon, he was summoned to the *schreibstube*. This thunderbolt warned me of the impending death of Witold, as well as of all the other officers.

I was shaken through and through. What could I do for these unhappy men except pray for them with all my heart? Not for their souls, for these were absolved by the priest's blessing, purified by their martyrdom. I prayed that those who were still alive might be granted two graces; as a Pole, I asked that they might preserve their dignity to the very end; as a human being, that their end might be as little terrible as possible.

In the evening my companions from the barracks related to me everything that had happened during that dreadful day. The barracks commandant had received the order in the morning, but he had kept it from everyone else. Before noon, the Colonel (Witold) was summoned to the Political Department. The Commander talked quietly and sensibly and expressed a wish to have him employed in the Department. This office work was what many a prisoner dreamed of, but Witold saw in this decision primarily the proof of a satisfactory outcome of his case in Berlin. He came back to the barracks delighted. A great burden had fallen from his heart and his thoughts.

68

What could have made this Gestapo man act in such a way? Did he want to have a look at a man who would be dead within a few hours? Play with him and cruelly mock him? Laugh at him in his heart? Or else was he moved by another, a 'nobler' (the pen is reluctant to write this word here), feeling? Was he anxious to give the doomed man a few happy moments? Probably not. But it was one of the favourite ways of Hitler's Germans to *tarnen*, disguise things, weave fiction, dress up with illusions. Those sentenced were sent out on to the wires, so that they might be killed 'while escaping'. Those who were to enter the gas chambers had a towel and a piece of soap thrust into their hands. Something of the kind must evidently have been applied to Witold. How terrible it must have been for him to become suddenly aware of reality.

In the afternoon when the clerk was fulfilling his ghastly duty, none of those who had been summoned lost his self control. They were full of courage, all of them. Each in turn sought the priest who, after a few words with them, gave them absolution and his blessing. The few Poles left in the barracks stood, that afternoon, huddled together, a helpless and desolate group, while clusters of Hungarians and Russians looked on in silence from further off. One more detail, painful to hear, was mentioned by my informants. For some reason, the carrying out of the sentence was delayed, and for almost two hours those about to die stood in front of the door behind which death was crouching.

A few days later, further information came from the most gruesome places in the camp – the death chambers, the mortuary, the crematorium. All these establishments, as everything else in the camp, were manned by prisoners who, after short periods of time, were destroyed in their turn as troublesome witnesses of all this. The sentence passed on officers was carried out by means of a shot in the back of the head. One after another had to stand in an apparatus which, by means of a movable opening, allowed for the shot to be fired at the exact place. The Deputy Commander himself, Lagerführer Bachmeir, who was said to have shot 8,000 prisoners out of hand, hidden behind a specially arranged wall, performed the duties of excutioner.

The bodies of Witold and the others were thrown into a mortuary under the hall of execution. A moment later, one of the attendants went there and saw the Colonel on his feet, looking at him with half-conscious eyes. The horrified attendant withdrew and Bachmeir dashed in and with a few shots finished off his victim.

The Polish tragedy was soon forgotten. The impression of death, by whatever means, was wiped out so rapidly. It was not of sentences carried out that one spoke, but of those yet to come. No more of them were passed on my friends, but how many were to die around me! All those who died from exhaustion had an easy end. They just passed out while asleep, went peacefully to the other world. I have not witnessed a really bad death agony; in the camp life was cruel, but death was kind – the consoler, salvation. Yet, despite the overcrowding in the hospital, men were dying in terrible loneliness, deserted, neglected. Sometimes I would make the sign of the cross on the forehead of one of my neighbours who was growing old, and this was the only thing that made the death of a man different from that of an animal. The warder would come, give a look, the rags were rapidly stripped off, the naked corpse left outside in front of the entrance door, whence, after a few hours or the next morning, it was taken away by prisoners to be put, like a large log of wood, with others into a stove which the Germans called crematorium.

I often used to ask after someone I had met and of whom, after a short period of time, I had lost sight. The answer frequently was "Oh, yes, there was a man like that. He went up the chimney a long time ago!"

Nowhere, on no battlefield, did life and death intermingle so brutally, so ridiculously, as in the camp.

For the Germans took care that life should go on normally. One could listen to good music and concerts, and on the football fields cries of enthusiasm followed a well-scored goal. Boxing matches were the most popular. This was after the taste of the SS men. A successful boxer became a prominent. The SS men eyed with approval a man who could knock down his opponent in one blow. They would try to gain practice in that art on the weakest prisoners. And simultaneously, co-existing with all these concerts, these sports, there was also that other life . . .

The Black Death had passed through Europe in the fourteenth century, devastating countries, depopulating cities. The chroniclers noted that after the first great wave of horror, people got used to it, almost fraternized with the terrible visitor. And a frenzy for pleasure took hold of many; they wanted to taste some joy and make good use of the day they still had to live before falling down in cramps, before becoming black. People drank and danced as never before, made love, threw dice and scattered Florentine gold. Something of that atmosphere pervaded the camp. Now, too, death, personified by the possessed madman of Braunau, ruled over Europe; once more it depopulated cities, devastated countries. But the people in the camps, herded together to die, no longer feared death and wanted to be carefree and gay. I remember a Saturday after roll-call in the hospital ward. It was the best moment in the week, for on Sundays no blood was spilled. A corpse was lying on one of the beds, but around it people were gay and not hungry, for the organisation had worked well, the stove was burning away so it was pleasantly warm, and the ward seemed cosy, filled with the babble of voices and jokes which went on until late at night.

Autumn slowly passed into winter. We knew that this was the last winter in the camp. We knew that the camp gates would soon burst open, but we did not know whether, for very many of us, those gates would burst open soon enough.

71

VII

STRANGE SYMPHONY

NOT long ago I was asked which incident, witnessed in the German concentration camp of Mauthausen, had made the strongest impression on me. In reply I described one particular occurrence and my questioner was greatly astonished because the incident related by me had nothing to do either with the camp authorities or with any of the numerous underlings of the regime who, dressed in SS uniforms, were doing their own share of cruelties.

This incident happened in the evening, after the last parade. One can compare the bell which rang at the end of this parade – if it were not impossible to compare the heavy sadness of the camp with the sunny days of school life – with the bell at the sound of which the boys in school feel relief and proceed to rest physically and intellectually. In the camp this bell was the sign that a certain number of hours of comparative safety were beginning. One was not safe, of course, from various torments – one was never safe from those – but from fundamental changes in one's fate like ˉbeing sent with a transport, transferred into a punitive company or called for execution. Even if a decision had already been taken in the office, one was notified of it and it was put into operation only on the next day after morning parade.

Now the guards and wardens, in crowds, had left for the main kitchen to fetch their suppers about which they had been worrying – discussing food – since early morning. We, the interned, meanwhile dragged ourselves, if not too weak, through the shadows of the narrow passages between the beds, occasionally stopping to talk. Outside, large snowflakes were falling damply and the icy wind was strong so that the guards were hurrying back through the length of the immense room to the comfortable corner of it which was allotted to them with long, energetic steps, their heavy boots clattering on the floor which shook under the weight of their bodies and of the large plates they carried with loving care. The plates, full to the brim, contained potatoes cooked in margarine or soup with sausages.

On the evening to which I refer, the time seemed to be going particularly slowly. It was already quite late, however, when, in a corner of the hut, I noticed a cluster of men, laughing and talking noisily. I approached them. The corner in which they were standing was the worst in the building. It was the corner of the wall behind which were located the more than primitive sanitary arrangements. On the beds in this particular corner – designated by a specially filthy German word – were thrown those from among us who – having gone through their pilgrimage in the camp, whether long or short, were nearing the hour in which they would be released, in camp language 'through the crematorium chimney'. On the thin planks and the ragged mattresses were human rags, awaiting their last hour in complete neglect, in an atmosphere of poisoned air coming from behind the wall and icy wind coming through the near and continually opened door.

The men who had attracted my attention were standing around a bed on which was sitting a man-skeleton, his head bound in a dirty piece of rag. This man was rotating continuously on his own axis, with a strange speed. His movement was accompanied by the uninterrupted shriek of a tormented human being. It was a shrill, high shriek, falling at times into a low wail, then returning again to its former shrillness. Now, the group of men who had been laughing with such delight, began to imitate this voice. In accompaniment to the voice of the dying man they were shrilly squeaking, their voices becoming lower when his did. Bewildered by this amazing scene, I looked at the victim of approaching death sharply outlined by the glaring light, and looked also at the men who, standing in the shadow, were thus entertained by suffering. Slowly I was losing the sense of place and time, forgetting the camp and the war, forgetting that I was the witness of death, so common now in the heart of Europe. I had the feeling of being in a part of Asia, perhaps still undiscovered, in some cave of Mongolia or Tibet, and of witnessing there a strange kind of ritual. The thinness and nakedness of the man, whose bald head was wrapped up in this ragged turban, the incessant rotation of his body, the voice unvarying in its double-tone chant, gave the illusion of some pagan priest celebrating a pagan service with the accompaniment of the crowd. Out of my imagining, however, I was immediately awakened when my eyes met those of the chief actor in what had seemed to me to be an exotic scene. The expression of his eyes, full of pain, was conscious. The suffering man saw and realised that the torment he endured was a diverting episode for these men whose voices he heard imitating his, the imitation differing, however, by its gaiety from the voice of agonised protest against his undeserved torture. His voice and theirs, sounding together, seemed like a symphony, a strange symphony of pain and derision, a symphony impossible anywhere except in such a concentration camp. And these men who were thus making game of infinite human suffering were not criminals or old convicts hardened by a life of crime. They were considered to be the best in our camp – young, healthy men with the red sign of political prisoners on their uniforms. Soon they were to return to their respective countries and there work as clerks or politicians or social reformers – some of them even as teachers to a new generation. One of them, I knew, had come to this camp as the result of a noble patriotic action of his own; and

74

now, before my eyes, his camp education was being completed.

When, after the signal for lights out had been given, I lay on the quarter of the bed allotted to me, crushed against the wall, unable to sleep, the thought came to me that although the Germans had lost the war, lost their towns, lost their powerful commercial achievements and their many beautiful old buildings, one thing they had not lost. They had not 'lost' their concentration camps.

IX

MR JOHNNY

THE first of March is not always a beautiful day, even under the sky of liberty, because, already long, it bears all the sadness of nature now devoid of winter's sparkling vigour and not yet rejoicing in the reviving breath of spring. But we who lived in the darkness of the hospital blocks were but little interested in the changes and shades of nature. So if I say that the first of March was a dismal day for me in Mauthausen I do not mean to accuse nature.

In the camp things always happened suddenly and without warning. All the orders and changes were impossible and illogical. To ask for information from the givers of these orders was madness, and even one's fellow prisoners were irritated if one tried to find out. "If they call you," they said, "grab your belongings and obey".

On this day I was ordered to move immediately from my hospital block. This threatened me with the loss of all my little personal possessions, most of them forbidden, without which endurance is all the harder. On being transferred into a new block an inspection was inevitable, and the individual in power took everything that might be of use to him or could be an object of barter. I was not too badly off, thanks to the kindness of my Polish, Hungarian, and Austrian companions and also to the cigarettes which I had been able to buy in the summer. The most important of my treasures were three sweaters. They had served me well in the camp hospital which was at a higher altitude than the rest of the camp, where I had been kept in an unheated ward with broken windows. The interminable shivering, night and day, was a most persistent cause of suffering in our punishment. Now, in the lower hospital, one did not feel the frost because each block was obliged to contain more than 1,000 persons, four of us being crammed in each bed some 75cm. (29½ inches) wide. Apart from the sweaters which I regarded now as precious capital to keep for the moment of liberation, I had still more things to lose.

Having parted in haste from my three bedfellows with whom I had been entangled by Fate for many weeks (and of whom two were to die soon after I left the block), I took a deep breath outside, looked at the yellowish grey sky, perhaps promising rain, perhaps fine, walked some distance through the slush and entered my new shelter.

Near the door stood a figure well clothed, well nourished – therefore an authority. I learned afterwards that it was Johnny, the substitute for the room overseer, whom some called Mr Johnny. All the capo-bandits had pet names. Johnny was between twenty and thirty. The Germans had transferred him from prison to Mauthausen where he was promoted to the rank of *capo*, in other words persecutor of his fellow-prisoners, and an extension of the SS punitive arm. He had only one arm, therefore the other was all the better developed for beating. Now, Johnny turned towards me and I beheld the most repulsive face in the camp (and there were plenty to choose from), his features displaying all the accumulated ferocity of the twentieth century since Christ. Now, he observed me with an eye which did not presage anything good for me. "Come here," he said. "Show what you have and take off everything". His voice was harsh, grinding. "What, what, what," he said with growing indignation, when from under my dark blue sweater appeared the brown one, and under it already peeped the green border of the third, called the SS sweater. "You, what's your age?"

"Fifty-nine."

"And you are so frightened of dying that you wear three sweaters?"

"I am not afraid in the least, but as long as I am alive why should I freeze?"

"Why, tell me, you, why? Then you . . . you don't know yet that you are now in the camp and you don't know, you . . . that you have no right to more than one sweater. This I will leave you." And he threw me the worst one. Besides the sweaters, Johnny took almost everything. I was ruined.

Now there came another official prisoner, fat and squat, resembling Sparafucile in *Rigoletto**, but the splendid indifference of his expression took away any hope of intervention in my favour.

"Come now," ordered Johnny. "I shall show you where you will lie."

We plunged into the jungle of bunks. What now surrounded me was already familiar to me from the other blocks. In an incredible mass, piled one on top of another, were decaying human beings badly covered with rags, many with wounds, many with deformities, many with swellings due to hunger. Some were lying motionless, others were sitting, staring, a strange conglomeration of human misery at its depths – a sight taken, one would have thought, straight from the Middle Ages at the time of the Black Death or of famine. I was reminded of a picture I had seen – St Charles Borromeo among the people stricken with plague – only here I could see no St Charles. The entire room could have been the hold of some huge Turkish sailing ship or Venetian galley which, in the sixteenth or seventeenth century, brought the slaves under the whips of butchers like Johnny. The latter now stopped beside a dirty nook and pointing low down ordered: "Here, with these three."

In my last block the bunks had been made in two tiers. Here they were in three, and the spaces between were so narrow that even a very small and young man would find it difficult to squeeze into one. The beds were named

*The assassin in Verdi's opera.

'coffins', but they were, in reality, more like drawers as they were so flat and, like drawers over-filled with objects, there were choc-a-bloc with bodies. Louis XI, cunning and cruel, liked to travel with his rebellious vassals in cages, but the vassal was alone in his cage and certainly had more light and air. How could I, with my great height, slide into this drawer, how manage the necessary actions, how eat my soup while bumping my head continuously on the boards above me, how jump out when chased to wash, to be examined for lice, when the supervisor would roar "All out of the bunks"? I looked into the gloomy depths of beds below, and from them glared with hatred the eyes of those from whom I would take away the heaven of sleeping only three in a bunk.

Meantime, Johnny had walked some distance away and stood observing me mockingly. I turned towards him and said firmly "I demand the highest bunk. I will not get in here."

"What? What do you say?" He burst out laughing, genuinely amused. "You will not get in here? But now we shall see." And lifting his arm, ready to strike, he advanced towards me. It was a critical moment. Later on, there were moments even more critical when we were called up several times a day to be selected for the gas chamber, but that was a question of death only, and a relatively quick death, not slow moral martyrdom. In our unceasing mental torment I often saw a welcome haven in the gas chamber because it would save us, once and for all, from all this. But what was to be done now? I had taken the decision not to obey. Was I to be beaten without resistance by this beast resembling a human being? Rebellion! That meant a punitive detachment, carrying heavy stones in the quarries under the bludgeons of the guards, or being thrown over the precipice.

Johnny was already at my side, but with him came an unexpected aid, as had happened to me at times in the most difficult moments ever since the day of my arrest.

Before me stood a young man with a pleasant face, saying politely in Polish with a Russian accent "Please Sir, come with me. I shall give you another place." He was a doctor, a white Russian, and therefore anti-communist. My new place had already three occupants, but it was the upper bunk and at this moment I was filled with the same joy and sense of freedom as the mountain climber on top of his beloved mountains.

The days dragged along painfully, in misery and degradation. Already the April sun rose above the camp and an occasional ray sought out the dark, sad corners of our prison. I welcomed joyfully these rays of sunshine as messengers from the Allied Armies, and they seemed to grow warmer around us as our deliverers came nearer. Yet in the last weeks the dangers accumulated greatly, bringing extermination at a more furious speed to the thousands already on the threshold of freedom, like snow melting before a hotter sun. I fought against the exhaustion of starvation only by the strength of my nerves which were to collapse immediately after the liberation and for a long time. From murder by gas I was preserved only by the grace of God in the form of a strange chance sending me back alone from a great number destined to be gassed but unaware of their fate. The subsequent selections for the gas chamber were made from among those who were already well informed. When the verdict spared me, I returned to my block with a certain relief, but fourteen months of familiarity with this or that form of death resulted in a feeling of satisfaction less than that experienced by a schoolboy on getting a good mark.

The third menace was the great likelihood of evacuation and consequent mass death for all those who could not advance. But Mauthausen had nowhere to which to evacuate and the choice of fate for this camp, rigourous even in comparison with other camps, proved a happy liberation.

At last, the marvellous day of 5th March arrived when

the American tanks reached us on the height of Mauthausen, for so long satiated with blood and ashes, the arena for so many years of physical and moral tortures. Everywhere in the camp where there still happened to be physically strong prisoners, unmerciful lynching had begun – the account between the slaves of yesterday and the butchers of yesterday. In our block, Johnny was wondering, anxious and bewildered. For him the good times and easy life had ended. When he was passing near my bed, like a wolf at bay, one of my companions asked him "Well, Johnny, I suppose now you will give me back my gold?"

"What gold? What do you mean, gold?"

"What gold, indeed! What about the two gold teeth which you took from me?"

"Untrue, I took nothing. Where is the proof? Where are the witnesses?" shouted the infuriated Johnny.

I joined in the conversation. "Calm yourself, Mr Johnny," said I with a politeness worthy of Versailles. "Now the Americans will enquire into everything so carefully that your innocence must be exposed in all its splendour."

Johnny looked at me suspicously, turned and went away. An hour later, no one could tell what had become of him.

Where can he be now? It may be that, having escaped through the barbed wire, he was absorbed by the Austrian countryside like so many bandits who fled the camps and, sowing terror everywhere, robbed, attacked and broke into houses, pressing the barrels of American pistols to the chests of terrified peasants. And it may be that Johnny, like those others, has at last reached a real criminal prison. This development I fear for Johnny but I do not wish for him. Because against none of those from 'There' do I feel any rancour, just as I would not feel it against the lightning which would burn my castle, or, if this comparison is too flattering, against a wild animal that might

81

attack me. I wish for Johnny that it would be given to him to find his soul . . . Then, perhaps, I could some day shake the hand which, on that gloomy March day in the airless hole of Hitler's galley, was raised punishingly over the resisting slave.

X

THE MORTAL CONTEST

THERE is a story handed down from the opulent Flanders of the Middle Ages. It tells of a drunken peasant found lying in a ditch by the merry-making courtiers of the Duke of Burgundy and transported to the castle chambers where, from his first moment of waking, homage and elaborate luxury were lavished upon him. At the banquet, the Duke himself, Philip the Good, raised his golden cup in a toast to the eminent guest. The simpleton ended by believing in his own greatness; and in the evening, when he was thoroughly drunk again, he was taken back by the courtiers to the very same spot in the same ditch.

The adventure of the Flemish drunkard really depicts the transient glory of many of those given the authority of *capo* in the concentration camps by the sinister rulings of the masters of the Third Reich. On the day of liberation the harshest of the *capos* were lynched, while those who survived must have experienced the same feelings as did the ducal guest of yore. For it was not every *capo* who was inhuman, yet each of them without exception prospered. They lived by drawing freely and in plenty the abundant food from the main kitchen, the choicest pieces stolen out of other people's parcels, excellent clothing, and a variety of articles from the stores. They had cigarettes and drink, slept in comfort, and – for a piece of bread or from fear – were served more diligently than ever a prince was in his own castle.

The most powerful *capos* were not those in charge of particular blocks but the ones who performed the central functions embracing the whole camp. Their names were known by all and remembered by many, as are the names of film stars or famous performers in the field of sport. "I play the first fiddle in the camp," one of them told me. "I can do anything."

Some of them, especially Germans, treated us – the grey crowd – with the most elaborate scorn. I would be underestimating their arrogance were I to assert that they looked at us with an air of superiority, or else did not look at us at all, for they just did not see us. We were thin air. Spanish grandees of the days of the Philips would have been outdone by their manner. Those in charge of the blocks all had a criminal record. They and the SS men strove to outdo each other in premeditated cruelty and were, in fact, masters of life and death to the common prisoners. There was a crazy, demented look in the eyes of these perverts. It was their unchecked and unhampered whims that created the so-called golden youth in German concentration camps. These young men – the very youngest – were beautifully dressed and pampered, their boyish good looks sometimes accentuated by cosmetics, and all were invariably adorned with a watch upon a delicate wrist. They were full of their own importance and showed it in their relations with other prisoners. They constituted a rich and characteristic chapter in the history of all German concentration camps.

I HAD spent the autumn months of 1944 in hospital, the first fortnight or so in a pleasant 'prominent' ward. Early in January, 1945, I was back in my barracks block. It was a severe winter. Those returning to the block were, as a rule, supplied with clothing, but as all the warmer garments had gone long ago, I was issued with only a threadbare waistcoat minus a lining. It was a test of endurance to have to appear twice daily at the roll-call in a severe frost. When it rained it was worse still. The very idea of changing one's clothes was preposterous, and a stove, when lit, warmed only the *capos*. Like a tree in the forest I

84

got wet and froze, thawed, got dry, and then wet again. The fact that this mode of life did not produce even one single cold, showed that the organism, mindful, as it were, of the bare impossibility of weakness, rallied its forces to combat the most formidable foe – sheer exhaustion due to hunger and discomfort.

One Sunday afternoon after the roll-call I went out to breathe some fresh air. It was still and mild, unstirred by the gusty chill of the usual January wind. A colourless sky hung like a curved roof over the multitude of dark, elongated barrack huts. The characteristic feature of this afternoon was boredom – but boredom in camp was a blessing, while all animation was unpleasant. I encountered a fellow-countryman, one with whom I had shared my prison cell in Hungary. I liked the way this heir to an historic name always held his fine head high and proudly. I used to know his father and admire his manners; now it was the son who would instinctively pass to my left or take my arm with discretion and solicitude every time there was a stone or some roughness on our path. A touch of Versailles in Mauthausen! He told me of his block leader who raved and inflicted punishment when his fad of keeping the prisoners' bunks clean could not be gratified for sheer lack of scraping and cleaning equipment. The fellow was also keen on games and if his underlings did not shine in the Sunday sports the whole block suffered. My own *capos*, also perverted German criminals, were invariably irritated too. They would roar and threaten us. Thus we walked on, discussing our small domestic problems, and parted after a short time, bidding each other a joyless goodbye.

To the square where we lined up for roll-call, one marched on deep, frozen snow. In the early days of February, I fainted one day while standing in the line. This could be dangerous, as the stretcher was sometimes tilted before reaching the hospital and the patient would then fall to the ground, often from an appreciable height.

If, having partly regained consciousness, he tried to break his fall, he would be punished severely for malingering. I was taken to the 'refuge' and laid in the corridor. A young Frenchman, a good friend of mine, was passing by. He often crooned to me *Sous les ponts de Paris*, and now, having sympathised with my plight, he returned with a large hunk of bread. Even a German took a liking to me and offered me one of his two spoons.

Several hours later, I was marched in a long column to the sick quarters, which comprised ten blocks. On the threshold I hesitated and stood still. I had heard many stories told of the sick-bay, but I had never expected to see this neglect, destitution, and degradation of human beings. Yet since the autumn there had been an improvement and no one was any longer sent to the gas-chamber. The sick died in considerable numbers, but were no longer murdered.

Thanks to the care of Polish doctors, I was allocated to a separate bed. But not for long. The Germans were evacuating Oswiecim (Auschwitz), Gross-Rosen and other eastern camps. Prisoners who had survived the ghastly journey were only fit for hospital. Our own camp, until recently containing 3,000 patients, now had to accommodate 10,000. Only several hundred deaths per day put a check on a still further increase in numbers. Lying on my narrow bunk in the company of three others, I dreamed of the days when I had only two companions. At night, to avoid the feeling of a cork forced into the neck of a bottle, I risked a fall by lying partly on the edge of the bunk. It was an edge that was both sharp and hard, but my exhausted organism came to my rescue and granted me several hours of sleep. The nights in these overcrowded conditions were an infinite tax on the nerves. Men who in the daytime had lived together amicably became, after the lights were put out, implacable foes. My own companions were reasonable and our nights peaceful, but the barrack as a whole I shall never forget.

The stronger, furious and roaring, charged like wild beasts in search of more room. The weaker, often covered with wounds and sores and now crushed and kicked, uttered piercing cries for mercy. From many places at once came that shriek in two tones – of wrath and of pain – until it seemed that the whole barracks was calling out in one mighty wail of despair. Then the gaolers with whips strove to bring silence. The darkness, the cries, the shadows stalking with whips to strike at random - that, indeed, was a horrible scene. Now and then a dull thud and a dying moan were to be heard. It was a victim being pushed off one of the higher bunks, never to rise again.

News from the battle-fronts, passed on in strictest confidence, was not always encouraging, and the more seasoned prisoners prophesied that the war would go on for a long time.

In March, our semi-starvation ration of food was cut, and then cut again in April. Death from hunger became a reality, the clear picture of which was constantly before our eyes. There were days when the usual 1/81th part of a loaf of bread was not issued, and all the nourishment received in the course of the day consisted of a spoonful or two of unsweetened 'coffee' in the morning and three-quarters or half a litre of turnip soup at noon. The mortality curve went up rapidly. Corpses – or, rather, skeletons – were piled up high at the entrance of every barrack block. The all-powerful sensation of hunger tormented both the body and the mind. The former felt its gnawing, physical pain, but the affliction of the mind was even worse. The idea of food never left one for a moment. One felt a tremendous desire for rich, heavy dishes. One's palate demanded their flavour. One saw food when one's eyes were closed. Hunger made it impossible to sleep much and when exhaustion did take the upper hand, shadowy forms in one's dreams beckoned one to heavily-laden tables.

Cannibalism resulted from severe starvation, though

none of the Poles fell into this extreme. There were four different cases of it. One cannibal sharpened his spoon long and carefully, then like a twentieth century Poliphemos he cut out the liver of a corpse and immediately consumed it. The camp authorities were impressed by these cases. Rations were not increased, it is true, but all the metal spoons were confiscated and, instead, one wooden one was issued between several prisoners. Fortunately there appeared other spoons on the camp black market, but they cost one to two cigarettes and these were so very essential for the purchase of soup.

I, myself, occasionally obtained cigarettes from the Polish assistance organization, and now and again I was sent some from the camp, outside the hospital. On one occasion I was even sent a ration of bread. This helped me not to lose all my strength and resistance although my weight dropped to a little over half the normal figure. The camp doctor on inspection exclaimed, observing the swellings on my face, "Please don't alarm us so!" I still remember the anxious expression in his eyes, for even bread was easier to find in the camp than sympathy.

There was now joyful news from the front, and we could hear the thunder of heavy guns. The days had the atmosphere of a race – a mortal contest – and one punctuated at frequent intervals by death in our midst. What other methods would the Germans adopt to outstrip the visitors and stop us being taken alive? Would it be an air raid, or would the camp be blown up? Even evacuation into the mountains of the Tyrol would be equivalent to a death sentence for most of us.

On the last Saturday of April the authorities of our block received instructions to select several hundred of the most feeble of the patients with a view to transferring them to a newly-appointed hospital. There, they were to have the daily rations increased to two one-litre portions of soup and one sixth of a loaf of bread. I was one of those detailed to go, and we stood in front of the barracks in a column, five abreast and ready to march. I was approached by a passing Polish prisoner. "And you, too, are going?" he asked. He looked thoughtful, and then said "I know nothing at all. This is only a hunch, but I don't like the idea of this new hospital. Do you want to go there?"

"Not in the least," I said.

"Well, in that case I'll see the *schreiber* and try to have your name struck off the list," he said. Some moments later he reappeared, beckoning, at the barrack entrance.

This encounter, and the words we exchanged, were the proverbial thread on which hangs human life. Very soon it became known that the other poor creatures, alas, had gone to the gas chamber.

Twice more that same day our fate was in the balance, and by this time we were fully aware of what was going on. Numbers were read out, and each individual was called to the good or the bad side. My own number was far down on the list, and I waited a long time. I was reminded of the class roll-call in my school-days, but then the suspense had been more acute, for life in the camp was well designed to dull one's senses. Sunday was a peaceful day, but on Monday it started all over again. The barrack scribe, who was Polish, did all that was in his power to ease up on his instructions by reducing the numbers that had been prescribed and delaying the despatch of prisoners. More than that he could not do. Those selected behaved placidly, for only a weak spark of life was left in them, and perhaps they still had some faith left in their luck. One German, only, wailed and cried out.

By Tuesday – it was 1st May – our ranks had thinned out appreciably and the risk to those remaining increased correspondingly. In the morning I received a parcel of clothes to facilitate escape in case of any emergency. But how was one to escape through the barbed wire, or where could one hide in the camp? We were lying on our bunks, waiting for the orderlies' high-pitched cries to call us to one more fatal roll-call, when the Germans occupying the bunk below mine were approached by a friend who, in a hushed voice, told them that he had just overheard on the German news bulletin that the army was ordered to abandon all resistance – the road from the West was open. Immediately and in a loud voice I shouted the news in Polish to those about me. Then – I could not recognise them! All the faces were changed, some weeping, others struggling with tears. In that moment the heavy weight of imprisonment, of the threat of the gas chambers, and of the hateful camp itself, rolled off our backs.

In recent days the gas chamber has once more been in use as a quick method of destroying damning evidence, but now word went round that it had been dismantled, having swallowed 1,600 sick in the last few days. In the afternoon I had a visit from the camp outside the hospital. In the confusion a distant neighbour of mine, a landowner from the south-eastern part of Poland, had managed to lay his hands on a car; he found some books, historical novels, in some office room, and on the way down he had picked some lilac. He threw down the heavy books and the light, scented flowers on my bunk, and opened his arms - to a free man!

Three weeks later I was sent over to the neighbouring camp of Gusen. (It was said that this satellite camp of the sinister name excelled in horror even Mauthausen itself.) In my new barracks I was well cared for by a number of friendly people, liberated now and prisoners no longer. I was still in a very exhausted condition. Here, also, I experienced a most joyous moment: a Polish Lieutenant-Colonel on leave from his unit gave me good news of my children.

In the middle of June all the occupants of our block of barracks were transferred back to Mauthausen. Mauthausen was becoming empty and depopulated. I strolled across the camp. To us it had been a moral battlefield. The now silent barracks stood in the sun, dumb witnesses of the past hideous happenings, but also of splendid qualities. I attended Mass said by a Polish priest in one of these barracks. When he appeared in his surplice and we sang a hymn, it seemed to transform this place - which had been a place of torment for so many years – into one of our village churches, and it was difficult to control one's emotion.

In the early days of July I was interviewed by a man despatched from the *schreibstube*, who announced that a car was waiting for me and that I was to pack and get ready to go. I could guess the reason. In the days when we were still under canvas I had received a visit from some old acquaintances, an Austrian and his wife, who had searched the camp for me. They had asked me to stay with them in Linz, where they lived. I declined the invitation on that occasion and also when pressed again at a later date. They had now decided to break my resistance by adopting the official procedure. In the clothing store I found two elderly Poles, one of them a priest. They searched helpfully and produced some of the least tattered rags. My last action in the camp was to say farewell to its present commandant. We were not unmoved. Saying goodbye to him was also saying goodbye to the camp, a past still raw, like a flesh wound, and a portion of my life crammed with new experience.

In an excellent hospital in Linz I was soon surrounded by the care of friends, doctors full of solicitude, and gentle nurses. I found myself alone for the first time in sixteen months. How silent and empty the hospital building seemed! Where was the eternal congested throng that used never to leave one, the bestial roar of the SS men, the hysterical shrieks of the *capos*? They had passed, and were to be heard no more. I was free. But how different was this freedom from the one we had expected! There could not be a freedom more sad. I could not help thinking of Poland and her tragedy. The words 'They that sow in tears shall reap in joy' came to my mind. What bitterness there was in the realisation that to the nation that had sown, not in tears but in almost unendurable suffering, it was not given to reap in joy.